Date: 9/11/13

658.4094 BUT
Butman, John.
Breaking out : how to build
influence in a world of

BREAKING OUT

HARVARD BUSINESS REVIEW PRESS
BOSTON, MASSACHUSETTS

BREAKING OUT

HOW TO BUILD INFLUENCE IN A WORLD of COMPETING IDEAS

JOHN BUTMAN

The web addresses referenced in this book were live and correct at the time of the
book's publication but may be subject to change.

Library of Congress Cataloging-in-Publication Data

Butman, John.
   Breaking out : how to build influence in a world of competing ideas/
John Butman.
      pages cm
   Includes bibliographical references.
   ISBN 978-1-4221-7280-3 (alk. paper)
   1. New products.   2. Creative ability in business.   3. Creative thinking.
4. Diffusion of innovations.   5. Entrepreneurship.   I. Title.
   HF5415.153.B885 2013
   658.4'094—dc23

                                                    2012046803

The paper used in this publication meets the requirements of the American
National Standard for Permanence of Paper for Publications and Documents in
Libraries and Archives Z39.48-1992.

CONTENTS

BREAKING OUT

1

THE IDEA
ENTREPRENEUR

I think it was the e-mails from TED that made it clear to me that we had a new kind of cultural player on the scene: the idea entrepreneur.

I had joined an online discussion group and, on an impulse, opted to receive daily updates on current TED topics. (TED, for those who haven't opted in, stands for Technology, Entertainment, Design, and refers to the famous talks.) The TED e-mails started arriving with the subject line Ideas Worth Spreading. I would scan the topics—ranging from the political (Why can't America have a political system comprised of professionals rather than career politicians?) to the philosophical (Who am I?)—and soon enough found myself wondering: Are these really ideas? Are they truly worth spreading? Who is trying to spread them? What are their motives?

These questions snapped into new focus some issues I had been exploring for many years. I have spent most of my career in the work of idea development and have also steeped myself in idea-related literature and thinking, from Fernand Braudel (*The Wheels of Commerce*) to Everett Rogers (*Diffusion of Innovations*) to the Gladwell-era spate of idea investigators.

A GLUT

The growing popularity of the TED talks made it obvious that the phenomenon of idea development and distribution was changing. First of all, the flow of ideas had picked up enormously in recent years. Ideas were spewing out of books and blogs, articles and e-mails, conferences and seminars, like never before. One small indicator of this trend that I found intriguing: many of my male friends, who had not been particularly avid readers, were joining all-guy book clubs and describing their discussions there as among the most meaningful in their lives.

Part of the reason for this pickup in the flow of ideas, of course, has been the growth of the ideaplex. That is my term for the profusion of activities, channels, structures, and technologies for the creation, distribution and consumption of ideas, from the tweet to the "eduinfotainment fest"—those events, from the Aspen Ideas Festival to the World Economic Forum, that bring together elements of academia, business, science, and technology in a new form of theater that is bigger and perhaps more relevant than Broadway. So, with that TED e-mail, I began to see that the ideaplex has grown so voracious in its hunger for ideas and so variegated in its forms of presentation of them that it has encouraged a massive response such that the supply of ideas, or what purport to be ideas, is exceeding demand—to the point of a glut.

Just as intriguing and significant to me was the role of the individuals, the people who were espousing ideas. It seemed that more and more of them felt *passionately* (as they often put it) about their idea. They were not driven, they claimed, by a desire for personal fame, financial fortune, positional power, or structural control over others. They did not wish to invent products or start and sell companies. Rather, their goal was to influence current thinking and alter behavior with regard to their particular idea. They wanted to go public with their idea— by which I mean stepping out from the status quo of their own lives—with the hope of breaking out with the idea—that is, differentiating it from current thinking on the subject. Ultimately, they wanted to make a difference, start a movement, change the world.

How did these would-be idea entrepreneurs intend to achieve their goals? They would do so through influence and persuasion and personal example. Their tools? Themselves. The stuff of their lives. Their expressions and actions. They would write, speak, engage in conversations, and—very important—*show how their ideas could be put to practical use.* They were prepared to devote their energies to these efforts, center their lifework around their idea, and even create an enterprise to carry on the work after their active period had come to an end.

Excellent. Admirable. But, as I have learned from my work of three decades, the idea business is a tough one, from start to finish. It's difficult to develop an idea and harder to express it well. It's tough to get people simply to *hear* your idea, and harder still to enable them to understand it in ways that come close to your intended meaning. To cause others to incorporate your idea into their thinking stream? Challenging. To change their behavior, even in small ways? Daunting. To make a difference? Start a movement? Change the world? Hard. Harder. Hardest.

And yet, people accomplish all these things, to a greater or lesser degree and with smaller or larger numbers of people, more often and more successfully than you might think.

MY PURPOSE

How the idea entrepreneur goes public, breaks out, and achieves influence (and how you can, too) is the subject of this book.

I am not so much concerned with how to generate ideas, because that is typically not the idea entrepreneurs' problem; they usually have an idea—or the makings of one—but are uncertain how to express, go public, and gain influence with it. Besides, there is plenty of good content available elsewhere on the topics of creativity, idea generation, and innovation.

Nor do I go very deeply into the tactical aspects of breaking out, such as how to put together a sequenced program of activities (When do I start tweeting? How much content should I give away?) or technical questions such as the advantages and disadvantages of self-publishing. That's because there *is* no template, all these matters change rapidly, and every case is different. It would be better for you to talk with experts on this or to catch up with the current thinking available in content venues that, unlike books, do not take a year or two (or more) to create.

Finally, I don't go deeply into the financial aspects of idea entrepreneurship in this book—that is, how to monetize an idea or create profit from it. That's primarily because making money is not the main goal of the idea entrepreneur. They want to gain influence, change thinking, affect behavior—and they can do these things without earning much, if any, money. However, many idea entrepreneurs make lots of money, into the millions, even if they do not earn on the scale of business tycoons and superstar entertainers.

What *do* I talk about? The essential elements that go into form-
ing an idea. What is needed to take an idea public. How ideas and
idea entrepreneurs fare in the ideaplex. How and why ideas break
out from others. How they influence thinking and affect behavior. How ideas and their creators fit into larger societal thinking
streams.

GENESIS

Before I get into all of those things, however, let me say that not
everyone with an idea wants to or should break out—which is just
as well given that we have an idea glut—and I offer my father as
an example.

Dad was an electrical engineer who spent his career at Lincoln
Laboratory, an MIT research and development center not far
from Boston. Inside and outside the lab, Dad was constantly coming up with ideas for how the world could be improved in one
way or another.

In the 1960s, Dad became fascinated with solar power and the
need for renewable energy sources. To express his fascination and
put it into practice, he built a rudimentary sun-powered water
heater—a rectangular box, perhaps three feet wide by eight feet
long, painted black on the inside, through which he ran several
switchbacks of copper water pipe—and mounted it on the roof of
our summer cottage, then hooked it up to the outdoor shower.
On a sunny day, it warmed enough water for a pretty good wet-
ting. The solar heater got people talking, but I didn't notice anyone else putting one on their roof, at least not then.

Dad continued to be fascinated by renewable energy issues
throughout his life. When he was in his eighties, he would regularly join my wife, Nancy, and me for Sunday dinner, and more

often than not he had a new idea he wanted to run by us. One of them involved a plan for replacing conventional lightbulbs with strobe lights, which, he argued, would save huge amounts of energy and, thanks to the persistence of human vision, would not affect the quality of illumination we experienced. He seemed so taken by the idea that I asked if he wanted to develop it further or perhaps write about it.

"No," he said with a sigh and a smile. "I just like talking about it."

Life at the Front End

In addition to the insights I drew from my father, who did not wish to break out, and my observations of all those TED speakers who do, my conception of this cultural player—the idea entrepreneur—derives from my own experience in the field of idea development.

My work involves helping individuals (and often their organizations) to tease out, shape, articulate, express, and disseminate their ideas. I now mostly specialize in the front end of the process, where the idea is still a great big ball of stuff and needs a lot of attention before it's ready to go public. I have also, over the years, been involved in the expression of ideas in many forms, including videos and multimedia pieces, speeches and live events, blogs and articles, and some twenty-five books.

In this capacity, I have engaged with an intriguing array of people, including corporate executives, social crusaders, expert professionals, impassioned amateurs, and framework-toting consultants. They have described my role variously as a thought partner, writer, creative director, incubator, and idea developer. (Also magician, which I am not.)

Most of the people I work with, as well as many I have only observed, have a model of the idea entrepreneur in their mind, composed of elements from a variety of real-life people.

One of these models, especially for businesspeople, is Tom Peters. In 1962, Peters, who was then a consultant with McKinsey & Company, went public as coauthor, with Robert Waterman, of a book called *In Search of Excellence: Lessons from America's Best-Run Companies*. It became a best-seller and suddenly Peters was everywhere—speaking, offering advice, telling his story, writing articles and many more books, and eventually creating an organization, the Tom Peters Company. Here we can see a distinction between going public, which many people do—simply by publishing a book or making a speech—and breaking out, which means that by going public you have created a response and achieved some amount of influence. Whether and how long it lasts, however, is another matter.

It was intriguing to watch Peters as he broke out. At that time, I was creative director at a communications company based in Boston. Many of our corporate clients, as well as some of our not-for-profit and individual clients, quickly latched on to Peters's idea of excellence. They wanted to make it the theme of their next conference, weave it into a speech, build it into their strategy. Excellence, it seemed, was inescapable.

I remember thinking: What the *hell* is going on? Who *is* this guy Peters? How is he making this happen? *Is* he making this happen? I saw that his model was different from those of other idea-driven people. He was more focused on practices than academics tend to be. He revealed more about himself personally than businesspeople usually do. He was good at expressing his idea, both in writing and in speaking, which is a rare combination. He had the attitude of a rebel but worked within the establishment.

Hmm.

In 1989 I started my own company, now called Idea Platforms, to concentrate on helping people shape and express their ideas—primarily, at first, through books. I was fortunate to participate in several projects that gave me an even closer view of what was involved in breaking out. One of these was a book called *Real Boys: Rescuing Our Sons from the Myths of Boyhood* (Random House, 1999), which became a *New York Times* best-seller and propelled its author, psychiatrist William Pollack, to international prominence as an authority on boys and men. Dr. Pollack's idea is that society casts boys in roles that do not reflect their true natures and, as a result, causes them, and society, no end of trouble, from individual depression and loneliness to public violence. I saw that Dr. Pollack operated in a very different sphere of endeavor (psychology) but followed a model similar to that of business-focused Tom Peters.

Hmm once more. ⼁

Exploration

At last, about five years ago, having worked with dozens of people who wanted to express an idea, go public, and break out with it, I set out to study the phenomenon more rigorously, and that work is the basis of this book. In addition to my professional experiences with clients, I did a good deal of reading and research, talked endlessly with friends and colleagues, and spent a lot of time thinking, synthesizing, and analyzing.

I also conducted exclusive interviews with idea entrepreneurs with whom I have not worked but who were kind enough to spend time with me and/or members of my research team. These include Cesar Millan, the world-famous "dog whisperer"; Mireille Guiliano, author of *French Women Don't Get Fat* and an internationally in-demand speaker and adviser; Dr. Andrew Weil, a modern proponent of the Hippocratic ideal that we have the innate power to heal ourselves, author of numerous books and creator of other forms of expression, and founder of an organization that combines not-for-profit and for-profit components; Blake Mycoskie, founder of TOMS Shoes, a company that is one of a new breed of idea-driven, for-profit enterprises created primarily to achieve a public good; Hannah Salwen, coauthor of *The Power of Half* and originator of an audacious approach to philanthropy; Bryant Terry, an author-activist-chef who seeks social justice through nutrition; Maria Madison, cofounder of the Drinking Gourd Project, who demonstrates that the idea entrepreneur can operate on a local level; and in India, Dr. Bindeshwar Pathak and Dr. Kiran Bedi, both of whom demonstrate how the idea entrepreneur model can be adapted in different cultures and situations.

In addition to these people, I conducted research into a number of other idea entrepreneurs whose stories appear in the book, although I did not interview them. These include Edward Tufte (expert in the visual display of complex information who has greatly influenced the design of some of our most successful content venues, such as the *New York Times* online); Eckhart Tolle (spiritual teacher and author of the multimillion seller *The Power of Now*); Amy Chua (author of *Battle Hymn of the Tiger Mother* and advocate of rigorous Chinese-style parenting); and Barack Obama (yes, POTUS 44).

Why did I choose to feature these people? First and foremost, because they fit the model or illuminated some part of it. Second, because I had gained information and insights about many of them, through exclusive access, that shed light on their methods beyond what they have explained in their own words. And, finally, because they represent a range of disciplines and professions, address different issues and problems, and have created distinct expressions, platforms, and enterprises.

My team and I have found that people enjoy pondering the question of who is and who is not an idea entrepreneur, and all kinds of candidates have been put forward, beyond those included in this book. The discussion is useful because it helps clarify the characteristics and distinctions and it usually ends up with a definitive thumbs-up or thumbs-down. Even so, the definition of an idea entrepreneur is flexible. Some people have some of the characteristics, but not all. Some take on idea entrepreneurship for a period in their lives and then leave it behind. The idea entrepreneur itself is an idea—a mental model—and, like any such concept, no single person fits it perfectly.

Humanizing

All this experience, research, discussion, and thinking has made it clear to me that idea entrepreneurs do something that seems simple, but is difficult: they humanize and animate their idea.

An idea is, after all, nonmaterial, nothing more than a pattern in our brains, an ideal of how things could be, a vision. You cannot simply hand an idea to the next person as you would a sandwich. People connect much more fully with an idea if they can come to know and understand it as they would come to know and understand a human being.

To that end, the idea entrepreneur essentially *becomes* the idea.

They give the idea a personality, which is largely their own. They give it a body, through their physical presence, their actions, and their behaviors. They give it a voice. And they enable it to breathe on its own.

That process may sound just as abstract as an idea itself but, as I hope you will see, it can be understood, embraced, and practiced by others.

MODEL

To understand this better, let's consider a person I think of as a prototypical idea entrepreneur: Henry David Thoreau (1817–1862).

As the reader no doubt recalls, Thoreau is the author of *Walden*, which expresses his idea that people should live simply and deliberately through the narrative of his personal experiment: living alone in the woods near Walden Pond in Concord, Massachusetts, for a little more than two years. Thoreau also lived his idea with a more pointed political purpose in mind, spending a night in jail as an act of protest against a government tax (and the war it funded). He wrote about that experience in *Walden* as well as in *Civil Disobedience*.

In the interest of full disclosure, I should reveal that Thoreau's example is particularly present in my mind because I have long resided in Concord, where Thoreau was born, lived most of his life, and died. Here we have a street, school, restaurant, club, a society, and many other things named after and for Thoreau. Much of his original material and a plaster bust of him reside in the Concord Free Public Library. He no doubt often sauntered by our house, which was built sometime before 1660 and had therefore been standing for some two centuries before he passed by.

Thoreau is not only a local figure, but a global one. *Walden* continues to sell and his ideas to have influence; although he is missing some of the elements of the twenty-first-century version of the idea entrepreneur, the main elements are there.

Fascination

First, foremost, and absolutely essential—and characteristic of all idea entrepreneurs—Thoreau's idea was born of a deep, personal, and unignorable (for him) fascination. I like to think that his fascination was with woodchucks—because he writes about them with a particular relish—but it was, more generally, with nature and his relationship to it.

Thoreau could not keep himself from thinking about and experimenting with the notion of living simply, deliberately, and in close harmony with the natural world. What is a simple life? How does one deliberately achieve it? The compelling nature of the fascination, the desire to understand it, and (eventually) the urge to argue its significance to others distinguishes the idea entrepreneur from those of us who have a fascination (as most of us do)—and may pursue a career or an avocation because of it—but don't make a mission of it.

What's more, the idea entrepreneur's fascination is always inextricably woven into the very fabric of the life, rather than being an academic interest, a pet theory, or a line of philosophical inquiry. Thoreau's fascination drove him to build a house with the labor of his own hands; to live alone there in the woods overlooking Walden from July 4, 1845, to September 6, 1847; to swim, plant, saunter, and observe nature and himself each day. Few of us so completely integrate our fascination with the daily progress of our lives.

The focus on practices distinguishes idea entrepreneurs from theorists and many academics, and the practices are an essential part of how they help people bring the idea into their everyday lives. In *Walden*, for example, Thoreau details many of the "how-to's" of the simple, deliberate, natural life: methods for building and furnishing a simple house, ways to keep healthy, and the best meal (rye) to use when making bread over an open fire.

The fascination, the life events, and the practices are the main elements of the personal narrative through which the idea is gradually revealed, formed, and clarified.

So, as I'll discuss in chapter 2, as an idea entrepreneur you must not only have a fascination, which may not seem such a difficult thing, you must also know what it is, which can be harder than it might seem. Just as important, you must connect your personal fascination to a larger, more fundamental, and relevant issue that many people can connect with. And, finally, to go public you must be willing to reveal your fascination and express it in ways that compel and influence others. This last part draws many people up short, because it is so exposing, risky, and irreversible. Think carefully before you set foot into the ideaplex.

Expression

Had Thoreau spent his time in the woods and left it at that, he might still be remembered as an interesting local iconoclast and naturalist, but he would not have become the internationally revered, generation-spanning, world-changing, idea-driven figure that he is today. That happened largely because he wrote *Walden: Or, Life in the Woods*, in which he expresses his fascination, engagingly relates his personal narrative, and brilliantly connects the two into a stream of stories, lectures, aphorisms, exhortations, musings, and practical advice.

It is through expression that the fascination, and all the material and experience that has accumulated around it and in support of it, snaps into focus as an idea. Before that, the idea exists in bits and pieces, notes and scribbles, slides and visuals, articles and blogs and tweets, talks and conversations.

Of course, Thoreau wrote a great many other things—his diaries run into the millions of words—but *Walden* is the work that matters most. It is the best-known, most-discussed, best-selling expression of his idea, and therefore it is what I call his *sacred expression*. Every idea entrepreneur must have one, but it need not be a book. It can be a talk (Al Gore's was a PowerPoint presentation), a course or workshop (Edward Tufte has conducted a one-day course for more than twenty years), a shorter piece of writing, a practice, a video or television show (Cesar Millan's *Dog Whisperer*), an emblem (a visual representation of the idea), or even, as we'll see, an object or piece of merchandise (such as the little house that Maria Madison championed or the TOMS *alpargata*).

Creating a sacred expression—in whatever form—is the signature act of going public and, if things go according to intention, to breaking out. Many of us have fascinations. Some smaller number of us act on them. And even fewer decide to deliver our fascinations into the world. Every idea entrepreneur does.

In chapter 3, I talk about the types of expressions that idea entrepreneurs employ; why it's important to create a sacred expression and to know which expression it is (it is possible to focus on the wrong one, which can be dispiriting); the synergies and differences between writing and speaking; and, finally, why it is that idea entrepreneurs still write books in this era of online expression, but how its role has changed.

Respiration

Fascination is fundamental and expression is essential to creating an idea and going public with it, but even together they do not necessarily enable an idea entrepreneur to break out and gain influence. A third element, respiration, is required. By respiration, I mean that the idea, once expressed, becomes animated. It can breathe on its own without the idea entrepreneur constantly puffing air into it. The idea is nourished by other people, grows, and spreads.

Respiration looks different for every idea and idea entrepreneur. Sometimes it develops rapidly, usually in response to the emergence of a sacred expression, and engages multiple audiences. This can be quite intense—I call it hyperventilation (Amy Chua's experience is a good example of this)—and it usually calms down after a while. Sometimes respiration builds slowly and engages a delimited yet involved audience. (This is the case with Tufte.) For a very few idea entrepreneurs, the respiration builds rapidly, engages millions of people, and goes along steadily for an extended period of time. (Respiration around Eckhart Tolle's ideas continues in a massive global soughing.)

Chapter 4 is devoted to a discussion of the ways in which an idea entrepreneur can encourage respiration and keep it going, why it is necessary for today's idea entrepreneur to be "bi-expressionary" or, better yet, "multi-expressionary," and why even those forms of respiration that seem negative—satire, rebuttal, and backlash—contribute to the process of gaining influence for an idea.

IDEAPLEX

Thoreau was able to become a prototypical idea entrepreneur because the essential elements of the ideaplex—the ones that idea entrepreneurs still engage with as they go public and try to break out today—were just emerging in the mid-nineteenth century.

Of great importance was education, which had become more widespread and available to more people, causing literacy rates to rise significantly. As a result, more people were accustomed to the ways of learning and were comfortable with, and interested in, ideas. Today, of course, education is compulsory for everybody in the United States, although the number of years of schooling required varies from state to state, and the literacy rate for people over the age of fifteen is estimated at 99 percent.[1] Here, education infuses everything. One of the roles of the idea entrepreneur, therefore, is that of educator.

Changes in technology also played a part. In the nineteenth century, the telegraph enabled, for the first time, virtually instant communications across the country, so that information and ideas could be more easily spread—creating the concept of the "mass" audience where none had existed before. (Thoreau was not a fan of the telegraph, suggesting that it would create a demand for "news" that would exceed useful supply; sounds familiar.) Plus, improvements in printing technology, which made it possible to more quickly produce large quantities of printed materials, further facilitated the phenomenon of the best-seller. (An early block-buster was *Uncle Tom's Cabin*, published in 1852.)[2]

Today, the Internet does essentially what the telegraph did, but blown out in every dimension. And the business of publishing is being reinvented once again, but, even with all its forms and manifestations—physical and electronic, trade-published, self-published, or collaboratively created—the idea entrepreneur still largely depends on a best-seller of some description (most-visited site, viral video, hit television program) to break out.

Finally, it was in the early part of the nineteenth century that an essential element of the ideaplex was invented: the lecture circuit. Known as the Lyceum system, it was originally designed to bring continuing education to the working class. Thoreau did a bit of speaking, but it was his friend and mentor, Ralph Waldo Emerson (1803–1882), who really latched on to the new thing, becoming perhaps one of the first Americans to make a living as a professional speaker. The eduinfotainment fest is the descendant of the Lyceum movement and an essential element of idea entrepreneurship today.

Technology also played a role in the creation of the lecture cir-cuit. The expansion of the railroad enabled the speaker to make more appearances in more places more often. Emerson, at the peak of his demand—from 1858 through 1872—lectured an aver-age of forty-seven times a year.[3] That's a full schedule, even for the twenty-first century idea entrepreneur.

Today, as then, the ideaplex and the idea entrepreneur exist in a complementary relationship, each one feeding and feeding off the other. The ideaplex of today is such a vast phenomenon that we accept it like the air around us and can scarcely see how well developed and fundamental it is to our society. It comprises, of course, the social and traditional media (although there really is no distinction between them any more), and extends way beyond them, to include our entire educational system, the burgeoning network of conferences and events, numerous forms of think tanks and professional idea generators, as well as untold numbers of informal idea-driven entities—from book groups to salons to professional get-togethers. There is nothing like this ideaplex in any other country, certainly not in China and not so robustly in India, and not even in western Europe, where outsider thinking is not so heartily encouraged and embraced.

Platform and Institution

The ideaplex allows for the creation of a platform, by which I mean a set of expressions that animate and reinforce one another such that respiration spreads still further and can be sustained.

Emerson built a platform, as much as one could be built in the nineteenth century. Not only did he make a deliberate decision to join the lecture circuit, he also came to understand the complementarity among his various activities. Not only could a breakout book lead to a speaking tour that would generate respiration and income, it could offer opportunities to gather material that could be grist for the mill for the *next* set of writings—and those books and articles could be constructed to reach new audiences that might be interested in attending the series of lectures that were based on those writings. To a remarkable degree, Emerson's activities fueled, reinforced, and animated each other. Idea entrepreneurs do exactly the same thing today—and they have video, Facebook, Twitter, and NPR to further facilitate the process.

When the idea entrepreneur successfully creates this kind of mutually animating and self-reinforcing platform of expressions, some then choose to take another step and build an enterprise designed to further the idea beyond the capabilities of the idea entrepreneur himself.

In chapter 5, I talk about how idea entrepreneurs often build such structures around themselves, the revenue streams they generate, the different forms the organization may take (from a one-person band to a hybrid entity containing profit and not-for-profit elements), and how a few idea entrepreneurs establish long-lasting institutions designed to carry on the work of the idea beyond their lifespans.

THE THINKING JOURNEY

Although Emerson and Thoreau were different in the way they expressed their ideas and took them public, they both contributed to one thinking journey, by which I mean a single idea that is developed by a number of people over a long period of time.

All idea entrepreneurs contribute, in their own distinctive ways, to a thinking journey not entirely of their own making. Although Emerson probably gained more influence for the living-deliberately idea during his lifetime, it was Thoreau who—through his personal narrative, expressions, and practices—is a greater part of the respiration that continues around the idea today.

This is what idea entrepreneurs do. And I must add here that the idea they espouse is not only a fundamental and human one, it also aims—to borrow a characterization from philosopher Friedrich Nietzsche (1844–1900)—"to do what is good for the preservation of the human race."[4] It is life affirming. This brings up the issue of "good" versus "bad" ideas, which is largely outside the scope of this book. However, one way to think about this issue is that idea entrepreneurs do not seek to exert power or gain control over others. They don't seek to gain influence for themselves through legal authority, physical force, or positions of structural power. They employ only the methods of influence that I describe here. Yes, idea entrepreneurs can certainly have their faults, but they tend toward vanity rather than mania.

Still, the question of value and worthiness remains. My e-mails from TED (I'm still in) are just the tip of the iceberg of ideas that flood into my e-mail in-box, course through my brain, and proliferate across the ideaplex. (Hey, if you get a chance, take a look at this five-minute video, read this 3,000-word article, or scroll through the 472 comments on this blog post. Really interesting!) The wording of the subject line of the daily update from TED—"ideas worth spreading"—is telling. It does not say that the ideas are worth considering or evaluating or putting into practice; the focus seems to be on getting them out there until they pile up thick as electronic loam. Ideas have become so easy to spread, share, and even claim (justifiably or not) that it has become hard to sort them out, difficult to evaluate them, tricky to determine where they came from, and impossible to retain them all. It has reached the point that we have to take deliberate action to escape the inundation of ideas that has become a standard feature of our lives.

But, despite the idea glut, the ubiquity of the ideaplex, and the annoying presence of many ideas that *don't* seem particularly worth spreading, I would not opt out. That's because, every now and again, almost miraculously, along comes an idea that does have great power and value. I find myself seriously considering this one, processing it, not forgetting it. It blossoms in my mind. It seems genuine, relevant, useful, true somehow. I want to share it with other people, and not just by sending a link—*you might be interested, check it out, pretty cool*—I want to talk about it, write about, breathe it in, breathe it out again, slightly altered and, I think, improved. This particular idea starts to affect how I think. When I make a decision, it sometimes factors in. I come to feel some participation in and ownership of the idea. It embeds itself in my mind.

This is the phenomenon of breaking out. And it is likely to have happened as a result of the efforts—the fascination, expression, respiration—of an idea entrepreneur.

Possibly you.

2

FASCINATION

A fascination is essential to your work as an idea entrepreneur, because it is the fundamental human element—a shared interest or impulse—that enables you to make a connection with other people. It is the source of your energy, the driver that keeps you going over a long period of time, the wellspring that you dip into over and over again.

Oddly enough, the fascination may not be obvious in the original living of it. It has surprised me that many would-be entrepreneurs *don't* know what their fascination is, cannot articulate it or have never tried, think it is one thing when it's actually another, or are just not ready or able to "go there."

To break out, however, the idea entrepreneur must find the fascination, connect it with a fundamental human issue, find ways to express it, and be willing to reveal it. This can be remarkably difficult to do even though the fascination is usually right there, often so obvious and essential that we overlook or dismiss it. It won't be found or defined by looking anywhere but inside yourself, in a search for iconic life moments and key revelations that have thrown the fascination into high relief and nudged you along in the development of the idea.

ICONIC MOMENTS

Childhood is often a good place to start.

That is certainly when Cesar Millan's fascination first became evident. Millan is the Mexican-born dog *meister* whose early identification with dogs propelled him to leave his native country, establish himself in America, and become the immensely popular world-famous "dog whisperer." He stars in his own television show, his books have sold millions of copies, and he headlines in one-man (and many-dog) events at major venues around the world. He has advised the famous and mighty, as well as the unknown and the ordinary, on their dog relationships. He is revered by dog owners and lovers everywhere, as well as dissed and doubted by some other dog experts, especially those of the veterinary community.

Wellspring

Millan has gotten along particularly well with dogs for as long as he can remember, as he told me in a conversation we had while he was at his Dog Psychology Center in Santa Clarita, California, and I was at home in Concord. He had just come in from his early morning run with twenty dogs. That sounds like a lot, but not for Millan, who told me he runs with as many as sixty-five dogs at one time—many of them pit bulls with histories of aggression— without the use of leashes or any kind of restraint.

Millan was born in 1969 in Culiacan, a city near the west coast of Mexico, and spent a good deal of time during his early boyhood on his grandfather's farm in a nearby village. His grandfather was a *campesino,* essentially a sharecropper who rented a parcel of land from a wealthy landowner and looked after cows and raised chickens.

"And always there, in the background, were the dogs, usually living in loosely formed packs of five to seven animals," Millan writes in his book *Cesar's Way.* The dogs "worked for a living" by riding herd on the cows, protecting the borders of the property, accompanying the women into the fields. "If any of the workmen left a hat behind in the field, you could be sure one of the dogs would stay behind to watch it until the qwner returned."[1]

The dogs had no names. No one trained them; they had no leashes. No one spoke to them; they responded to a whistle. Now and again the dogs would get a burrito for their efforts, but mostly they scavenged or killed small animals to eat.

None of this seemed unusual to Millan, because he had not experienced any other human-dog environment. What was unusual, however, was the uncanny connection that Millan had with the dogs on the farm. This did not sit well with other people. He was "not a popular kid in Mexico," Millan told me. "I was called El Perrero." The dirty dog kid.

In our conversation, it struck me that Millan spoke about those early days in Mexico as if they were yesterday. This is a reliable indicator of a fascination: no matter how ancient it may be, it has a powerful immediate presence. It is always right there, waiting to be tapped.

Catalyst

If you had asked Millan at age five or ten what fascinated him, he might have replied, "dogs"—or he might not have. Either way, his connection with dogs might never have amounted to anything more than that had his fascination not been brought forward—tested, ignited, propelled toward an idea or an action.

For Millan, that catalyst arrived when Millan was still quite young. His father moved the family to the city of Mazatlan, a couple hundred kilometers to the west. When the Millans got a television set for the first time, it didn't take long for Millan to happen on some American-made shows. Some of his favorites were, not surprisingly, *Lassie* and *Rin Tin Tin*.

Millan was riveted, and a little perplexed. The dog-stars behaved like no real dogs he knew. When their human beings talked to them, the dogs seemed to understand and do their masters' bidding. How was this possible? Were the dogs different? Were their trainers wizards? "That inspired me," Millan told me. "I said, 'I've got to go to Hollywood so I can learn from Americans how to do this.'"

But he was only thirteen or fourteen and had no money. So he worked in the office of a local vet, which was a combination of doctor's office, groomer, and kennel. At last, at the age of twenty-one, on the day before Christmas 1990, Millan announced to his mother that he was leaving for America, that very day. Why? He intended to become the best dog trainer in the world.

"What was going through your mind at the time?" I asked.

"You don't question a feeling," Millan said. "It's one of the things that people like myself drive themselves with. Some people can call it fate. Some people call it instinct. You can't eat, you're getting nervous, anxious. It's almost like a vision."

I would call it a fascination, aroused.

Leaving

Millan could have stayed in Mexico, I suppose, and created a life as a dog trainer there, but the idea entrepreneur almost always undergoes a meaningful act of *leaving*. The fascination must be strong enough to propel you to a new place and, in the process, to leave something familiar, expected, comfortable—a country, an institution, a job or career, a discipline. Idea entrepreneurs are often outsiders, in some way, or make themselves so, at least for a time.

Millan's leaving was extreme: home, country, language, and family, as well as his old idea of what dogs are and how they relate to human beings. He crossed the border, without papers, and made his way to San Diego. There, unable to find a job, he lived under the freeway for a time.

This became a period of observation and accumulation of material for Millan. On the streets, he had plenty of time to watch the behavior of Americans and their dogs. What he saw struck him as very odd. People were supposedly walking their dogs, but in fact their dogs seemed to be walking them. "Wow," Millan thought to himself. "Nobody does that in Mexico. Nobody puts a leash on a dog, period, on a farm. Something's wrong here." An idea had begun to form in relation to his fascination: in this country, the relationship between these two creatures is fundamentally out of whack.

Finally, Millan got a job at a dog grooming shop, because the owners sensed something special about him. When he had gathered a little money, he moved to Los Angeles, where he found work with a dog trainer. There he got to observe the training methods that he imagined had produced the behavior of Lassie and Rin Tin Tin. Millan saw that the dogs were no different than the dogs he knew in Mexico, and the trainers were not magicians at all. The trainers seemed to think of the dogs as robots, not living creatures. Their methods consisted of tricks, treats, and mechanical devices, including leashes and collars.

The job also gave Millan the opportunity to talk with the dogs' owners and observe them up close. He learned that Americans showered their dogs with affection, kissed them and cooed at them, dressed them in clothing, fed them human food, allowed them to sleep in their beds, and seemed to expect the dogs to respond as if they were four-legged people. When the dogs behaved badly (biting, chewing, being aggressive or exhibiting territorial behavior) the owners brought their dogs to the trainer to be corrected.

Millan developed his own techniques, based on his years of being and working with dogs, to bring the dog and human into a natural pack relationship: the human as the ascendant leader of the pack and the dog as the willing follower. "Calm assertiveness" as he came to call it. Gradually, people who came to the trainer where Millan worked, and saw how he related to dogs, began asking for him.

By 1994, four years after arriving in the United States, Millan had saved enough money and established enough of a reputation that he was able to open his own operation, Pacific Point Canine Academy, which soon gained a following. The word was out that El Perrero was able to connect with dogs in ways that no other trainer in Los Angeles could.

People could sense Millan's fascination, saw that his practices worked, and liked what he had to say, but the idea was still not fully articulated or expressed yet. That would come later.

FINDING

Cesar Millan was fortunate, perhaps, that his fascination was so obvious to him. Or was it? It is obvious now, because he has talked and written about it so extensively. But, as we'll see, that process of writing and talking about a fascination, in fact, serves to *make* it obvious. Millan began, remember, wanting to be the best dog trainer in the world, not a dog "psychologist," as he now calls himself. The understanding of one's fascination changes over time.

So perhaps it is not so surprising that many would-be idea entrepreneurs do not know what their fascination is or are unable to articulate it. I have seen the proof of this many times when I ask a client a few simple questions. What is driving you to go public with this idea? Why do you care so much about it? What got you interested in the first place? (I don't ask, "So, what's your fascination?" This will set the fascination's antennae to quivering and it may choose to protect itself in all kinds of disguises.)

The questions, although innocent and direct, often produce— from smart, articulate, and usually coherent people—rambling, stumbling, and even incoherent responses. This is not unusual and it does not mean that the person has no fascination, no idea, and no chance of breaking out. It just means there is some work to be done.

An Exercise

To help my clients get closer to their fascination, I developed an exercise that I call, not very cleverly, "fascinations." It's so simple and obvious that it hardly seems to be an exercise at all, which is one of its virtues—you cannot prepare or devise any kind of winning strategy, because there is no competition involved.

Usually the exercise works best when we have reached a state of being that I call "lost in the forest." The idea seems confused. The motivations have become uncertain. The accumulated material is mounting up but seems like it is just a great big ball of stuff, with little cohesion.

This is when I bring up the subject of fascination. "I'm not sure," I say, "what it is that really fascinates you about this subject." The reaction to this is often surprise. *Really? Haven't you been paying attention to everything I've been saying so far?*

"Yes," I reply, "but, still, we all know the idea isn't perfectly clear yet. I have found that this fascinations exercise can help." The client, frustrated or desperate, usually agrees. *Just to humor you, John.*

We sequester ourselves in a room, with little more than a whiteboard or a flipchart and a glass of water.

Here's how it works. I ask you to tell me what fascinates you about your idea and I write down whatever you say. Note the word *tell* here—I do not ask you to *write* your fascination in any form. You have to *talk* it out. This is partly to avoid any issues you may have with writing—the inhibitions, the blocks, the worries that other people will read what you have written, as well as the rules about grammar and spelling that have oppressed you since third grade. The talking is also important because it causes you to reach into memory in a different way than writing does and it enables you to see, immediately, what it is that affects other people (in this case, me) about your fascination.

When I describe the assignment, my client will typically groan a bit or good-naturedly roll the eyes.

"Haven't we been through this a hundred times already?"

"Yes, we have."

"So what do you want me to say that's different?"

"I want you to forget everything we have discussed," I explain. "Ignore everything we have articulated so far. I want you to tell me what is it about the idea that fascinates you *right now*. Not last week or last year. Right now in this room. Here. At this very moment."

The client gulps and looks nervous. This feels vaguely like psychotherapy. Or an acting exercise. An uncomfortable exposing of the inner self. Which is exactly what it is, although I don't say so.

"And I want to know what it is that fascinates *you* about the idea," I continue. "You personally. Not what you think fascinates your colleagues or your peers or the media or your significant other. Not what you think might fascinate *me*. What fascinates *you*."

Tiny beads of sweat begin to form. "Me?"

"You. And furthermore," I continue, "I want you to tell me what it is that *really* fascinates you about the idea, not what you think *should* fascinate you. Not what you have been telling yourself for the past month or year or decade that fascinates you. Not what others have been telling you *they* think fascinates you."

Tension exhibits itself around the eyes and in the shoulders.

"OK?" I ask.

It is obviously not OK. But there is usually a game response. "Sure."

"So, let's begin," I say, reaching for a marker.

Then the person has a natural, almost uncontrollable, reflex reaction. He or she lunges for an iPad, briefcase, notebook, or phone.

"I have some notes," they say. "I've already got this written down."

"*No notes!*" I bark.

"No notes?" The person freezes, hand on phone, fingers clutching the notebook, laptop screen half raised, a look of pain and wariness on the face. *No notes?*

"No notes." I repeat. "You don't need notes. You know your own fascination. Just tell me whatever comes to your mind. Things that fascinate you about this idea. About your endeavor. Let's go!"

Deep breath. "OK. OK, John." They begin to worry that I may be a bit deranged. "So, you want to know what fascinates me about the idea right now? Is that right?"

"Yes, I do." I express a teeny bit of exasperation, as if I might indeed be deranged and on the brink of eruption.

The client stalls for time. "OK. Umm . . . Let's see . . . "

The words, at last, start to come. The first few responses are usually predictable, as if the person is trying to reconstruct what's in the notes, grasping for the right answer that I, or somebody, will praise them for. No matter. I scribble the thoughts on the board, with no comment.

After those first few rote responses, the person may run a little dry, and we sit in awkward silence. That's fine. I let the silence continue, because something is happening. The person is going deeper and the fascination is starting to well up.

"What else?" I ask. "There's more, I'm sure."

A few more things come dribbling out. They seem a little different from the earlier responses. It's as if the tap has been opened and the first stream of water ran rusty, but now the faucet is gurgling and spitting.

"OK," the person says, at last, as if finally realizing that the true fascination is demanding to be acknowledged. "You want to know what *really* fascinates me?"

I smile. "Yes, that is precisely what I want to know."

And then there comes some kind of preface or caveat or disclaimer.

"Well, I mean this might sound kind of weird, but . . . "

"That's fine. There is no audience here. We're not recording."

Genuine

And then out comes the first clear drop of water, the genuine article. "What really fascinates me is . . . " Now the floodgates open and the fascination pours out—the voice free, the shoulders relaxed, the eyes gleaming—in drops and spurts, until the well has emptied itself. The session rarely lasts more than an hour, and the responses rarely fill more than a flipchart page or two. But that exercise can alter the course of the endeavor and influence everything that comes after, because, once revealed, the fascination can never be forgotten. It becomes unignorable, a touchstone.

I will not forget one session, involving two clients and two of their colleagues, in which something particularly amazing happened. We had been working together for at least three months, off and on, talking about and shaping the main idea. We had developed long lists of topics, created dozens of documents, and transcribed many hours of conversations. We reached a point, however, where we lost our way. The material seemed flat, the idea irrelevant, the motivation uncertain.

At last, we did a fascinations exercise. It went well. Energy. Excitement. After an hour, when we looked through the responses, something extraordinary struck me.

"Did anybody notice," I asked, "that not a single one of the topics we had all agreed were the most important ones—the messages and articulations and stories we had included on our lists and in our slides—showed up on the list of genuine fascinations? Not one."

From that moment, the old idea was abandoned and a new one began to emerge, built around the fascinations.

REVELATIONS

Some idea entrepreneurs have fascinations that are almost visceral, possibly ingrained in the DNA, as Millan's was (*Some people can call it fate*, he said), while others' fascinations show up—and perhaps are formed—through experiences and revelations without which things might have gone differently. These, too, can be discovered.

This, I believe, is how it happened for Mireille Guiliano, author of the *New York Times* best-seller *French Women Don't Get Fat* (Knopf, 2004; some three million copies sold worldwide[2]) and three other books (with two others under contract), writer of articles and blog posts, an internationally in-demand speaker and adviser, guest celebrity at special events, mentor to young women, and also a nascent movie person—Hilary Swank bought the film option rights and, although the option lapsed, a screen version of Guiliano's book is still a possibility.

Guiliano's idea is that people, especially women, can achieve and sustain good health (physical, mental, emotional, and psychological) as well as an attractive body—if not necessarily skinny, glamorous, or "perfect"—by following traditional French ideas about food, eating, and the joy of daily living, *joie de vivre*, rather than relying on diets and deprivations, torturous regimens or extreme exercise routines, medications, or medical interventions.

Her idea stems from a fascination that could be bluntly, if reductively, but not surprisingly stated—given the title of her book—to be: fat. This Guiliano explained to me and my colleague Anna Weiss when we met at her apartment in New York one rainy spring day. Guiliano, as Anna and I immediately observed (and as you might expect), is not at all fat, but neither is she socialite skinny or health-club buff. She was charming, natural, helpful, and made sure that we were well hydrated during our three-hour conversation.

Guiliano once *was* fat, however, if only for a brief time when she was a young woman, and that experience is the wellspring of her fascination, a key part of her personal narrative, and at the very center of her idea.

Helping

Guiliano was born in Moyeuvre-Grande, a village in northeastern France, in 1946. As a child, she did not have a weight problem. She was a normal, healthy, slim-enough girl. Yes, food played a featured role in the family's life. Guiliano's mother owned and operated a storefront shop, offering a variety of specialty food items. Guiliano was therefore perhaps more engaged with food, and more exposed to the connections different people had with food, than she might have been had her mother been a teacher or executive or something else.

Another important element of Guiliano's life was social responsibility. When she was in her early teens, her mother sent her off to a camp that specialized in doing good for others. One summer Guiliano helped paint the apartments of the elderly in Austria. Another year she worked on a farm in Yugoslavia. "It was very, very tough and we worked long hours," Guiliano told us. What's more, the food there was "really terrible."

After a few summers of this, Guiliano had had enough. Near the end of her junior year in high school, she said to her mother, "This year, I'd rather not." Her mother did not yield, explaining that it was very important to do things for other people and that, through the camp, Guiliano would have done more for others by the time she turned twenty-one than most people do in their entire lifetime.

"Someday," her mother said, "you'll get it."

This may have been a miserable moment for Guiliano at the time, but it became iconic for her much later, because it served as the motivation for eventually going public, as we'll see. In addition to the impulse of the educator, the idea entrepreneur also typically has this urge to give back, do good, to help others—to change the world in a life-affirming way.

Hurting

Many mothers have taught many daughters that helping people is important, and Guiliano might well have called it quits in the helping department at age twenty-one, had she had not experienced an act of leaving, that involved—like Millan's—a different country, a new culture, and an unexpected encounter. Millan's was with dogs and their American owners; Guiliano's was with chocolate chip cookies and the people who baked them.

In 1965, Guiliano was chosen to attend her senior year of high school abroad—in the town of Weston, Massachusetts, a suburb west of Boston. This had not been part of Guiliano's plan. As it happened, the family of the girl who originally had been chosen to go was revealed to be Communist. The organizers determined that, in the Cold War era, a young Communist would not be the ideal representative of France in the United States. So, Guiliano was selected to go in her stead.

In America, Guiliano developed a new and very un-French relationship with food. This was partly because she did not settle in with one family, but rather lived with a succession of families—six in all during the school year. In each home, the family members wanted her to experience the American lifestyle at its truest and most authentic, which, among other things, meant treating her to the native delicacies: chocolate shakes, chocolate chip cookies, brownies, and lemon meringue pies.

"All the wrong things!" Guiliano said to Anna and me.

Guiliano might have been able to handle all that food without letting it get to her mind or waistline, had it not been for the stress she felt about living in America. She hadn't chosen to come, after all, and she found herself acting as a kind of de facto French ambassador, even being cajoled into speaking at Wellesley College about her experience. "I was a nervous wreck," Guiliano said. Gradually, she started to use food as a way to deal with her anxiety, relieve stress, and provide a form of solace when she missed her home and family.

Guiliano accumulated weight, just as she would accumulate material about the effects of troubled eating later in her life. She didn't really notice the pounds piling on, however, or at least didn't allow herself to notice, until that spring, when she got out her shorts and tried to pull them on. No go. "I looked at myself in a full-length mirror, and it was bad," she said. When one of her host families whisked her off to their summer place on the resort island of Nantucket, the reality hit her full force. She realized, "Oh my god, I'm going home in six weeks, and it's bad." Guiliano had gained twenty pounds over the course of ten months. On a young woman who stood about five foot four, and whose optimal weight was around 115, that's a lot—almost a 20 percent increase.

It was an iconic moment for Guiliano, and one that oh-so-many people can identify with, including me. I remember putting on weight in my forties and one day pulling on a pair of pants and wondering, "Why have these pants shrunk?"

Something, she realized, had gone badly wrong with her relationship with food. Still, twenty pounds is hardly a fatal amount. Surely, a young person, with a bit of dieting and a little more exercise, might shed that much over the same period of time it took to put it on. But, of course, that is not what happened.

Instead, along came another iconic moment that made matters even worse.

Being Helped

At the end of the school year, Guiliano returned home by ocean liner (which can't have helped her calorie intake either), eager to be reunited with her family. Her father met her at the port in Le Havre, took one look at her new outline, and said that she looked like "*un sac de patates.*"[3] (Yes, a bag of potatoes.) Guiliano was stunned. She knew she had gained weight, but it wasn't really her fault! It was the anxiety. America. The brownies. The families and their hospitality. Her longing for home. How sharper than a serpent's tooth it is to have a too-frank parent!

That fall, Guiliano went off to Paris to attend the Sorbonne (the first of her family to go to college) and again felt the stress of new surroundings and unfamiliar routines, and again fell into the groove of her newly acquired habit—she ate. The route from her apartment to her classroom was lined with pastry shops and cafés, and she could not resist stopping in each morning.

By the time Guiliano returned home for the holidays in December, she had put on ten more pounds and was thirty pounds over the weight she had been just a year and a half earlier. She could no longer ignore or explain away her problem. She was miserable and looked it. Her mother saw that action was required. She prevailed on a family friend, Dr. Meyer, who was knowledgeable in matters of weight and attitude, to intercede. He came to visit, sat by Guiliano's side, and said, "Mireille, I've missed you. Tell me, how was America? How is your life in Paris?"

Guiliano burst into tears.

"What's the matter?" Dr. Meyer asked, knowing full well what the matter was.

Guiliano told him about the eating, about the complexity of life in America and the stress of college in Paris. Dr. Meyer patted her hand. "Mireille," he said, "we're going to do this together. It's going to be so easy. And I guarantee you by June you can fit into your bikini and you'll be on track again."

That is exactly what happened. The pounds melted away. By the following June, the bikini fit again. And Dr. Meyer, whom Guiliano refers to in her book as Dr. Miracle, had done little more than remind her of the essentials of the traditional French lifestyle: moderation, responding to the cues of the seasons, focusing on the pleasure of eating. He suggested a number of practices to her, including eating healthful quantities of leek soup.

Guiliano's personal problems with fat were over, but her awareness of weight and how it had all happened to her lingered. For the next forty years, she gathered all kinds of relevant material—experiences, ideas, facts, stories, references, images, insights, observations—thinking (consciously or not) that someday she would put it to a greater use.

ACCUMULATION

I call this collecting and gathering of material *accumulation*, and it is essential to the idea entrepreneur. Thoreau spent years gathering material, writing in his diary, wandering the woods of Concord, living two years alone in his house by the pond, all the while observing and gathering, sorting through, accepting and rejecting, organizing and categorizing, shaping and polishing material. Millan had been thinking about and interacting with dogs since he was a kid.

The accumulation of material may be methodical or haphazard, and it often comes to resemble that ball of stuff—a contangulation of notes, recordings, speeches, writings, clippings, links, videos, images, e-mails, PowerPoint decks, doodles, and scrawled-upon napkins, as well as mental notes and memories. Crammed computer folders. File cabinets bursting. Floors strewn with piles of whatever.

This is all good. The idea entrepreneur can only animate the idea when he or she knows a great deal about it—much more than most other people—and knows it in a personal and intimate way. Gathering this kind of knowledge is usually a different process from that of the journalist or the consultant or a member of the commentariat, who may well steep themselves in a topic to the point of impressive knowledge, but for whom the idea is not necessarily a central fascination or their lifework. They may move on to some other subject and start some new course of accumulation. The idea entrepreneur never leaves the fascination behind.

The importance of accumulation may seem obvious, but I have been approached by many people who want to go public with something resembling an idea and who assure me they have lots of stories to tell, a ton of material gathered, many insights to impart, plenty of great data—but somehow it never materializes, or there is not enough of it to fill a book or even a talk, or there is not enough that is original to the idea entrepreneur. It is not sufficient to simply regurgitate, in slightly altered form, a mass of borrowed material and reformulate the ideas of others, attach your own labels to it all, and expect people to respond. (I'm not talking about plagiarism here, just a lazy kind of synthesis.)

It is during this period of accumulation that something else is happening: the idea is beginning to emerge, take shape, and gain clarity in a kind of idea-making alchemy. The iconic moments and revelations of the fascination burble to the surface and interact with the nuggets of content. To that mixture, we add some number of trial expressions—bits of writing, talks, videos, graphics—as well as the trying-out of practices.

All the while, the idea entrepreneur is doing some thinking of a more conceptual nature: synthesizing, analyzing, identifying principles and themes, settling on key words and phrases, developing frameworks, and—very important—articulating (or at least trying to articulate) a single sentence that encapsulates the idea.

Frameworks

As important as the fascination and its iconic moments are, the idea entrepreneur must also have a framework of some kind that enables people to understand the idea in the abstract, as a general model, against which they can understand and analyze specific narratives and situations. As the old saying goes, "That's fine in practice, but will it work in theory?"[4]

A framework is a structure of the idea and usually contains a limited number of key elements that are basically descriptive in nature, such as principles, characteristics, parts, or themes. A framework may also include a number of elements that are more prescriptive, such as strategies, methods, rules, and the like.

Aristotle (384–322 BC), for example, developed a framework of stage tragedy in his work, *Poetics*. He describes six elements that he argues are essential to the composition of a successful tragedy. These he lists in order of importance, from plot (most important) to spectacle (least). Within each of these parts, Aristotle offers more detail on methods and practices; for example, the play should have a beginning, a middle, and an end, and the plot should be unified—each incident should be necessary to the larger story.[5] Aristotle's framework has held up well for more than two thousand years.

The elements of a framework may also be structured as an order, but it may or may not be order of importance. In 1943, Abraham Maslow (1908–1970) proposed his theory of human motivation, which is generally referred to as a "hierarchy" of needs—some are higher, some are lower, but all are important. The framework describes five human needs, which are ranked from the most basic physiological ones (e.g., food, sex, sleep) to higher-order needs related to esteem (e.g., respect) and, beyond that, to a state known as "self-actualization" (including creativity and capacities).[6] Maslow's hierarchy is often depicted as a pyramid, with the physiological needs at the bottom and self-actualization at the top, although Maslow himself did not present it that way.

Part of Stephen Covey's success is the strength and clarity of his framework. Its elements are called habits and they are arranged in a sequence of practice—what should be attended to first—rather than of importance. (Like Maslow's needs, Covey's habits are all important.) What's more, the framework is plainly stated right there in the title of his seminal book, *The Seven Habits of Highly Effective People.*

Covey's seven habits—the first of which is "be proactive" and the final is "sharpen the saw"—are organized into three parts: independence/self-mastery, interdependence, and self-renewal.[7] The framework effectively encapsulates Covey's idea that success is a matter of character that stems from following a set of replicable habits. The framework is clear and simple to remember; I have met more than one person who can rattle off all seven habits from memory, sometimes in order.

Seven Habits was published in 1989 and its framework became the basis for Covey's work of more than twenty years, and a major source of his influence. It is estimated that over twenty million copies have been sold.[8]

Lists

Frameworks are beloved by academics, philosophers, and business strategists, but simple and durable ones are very difficult to create—especially when it comes to the relationship and ordering of the elements. Which one is the most important? Which one comes before which others?

So the would-be idea entrepreneur will sometimes settle for creating a list of the elements of the idea, without worrying too much about relating them to basic principles, ranking them by importance, or sequencing them by execution. The list may be of interest, but it doesn't offer much in the way of theory, as a framework does, nor does it provide a helpful model for action.

Benjamin Franklin, one of our earliest idea entrepreneurs, found this out the hard way. Franklin's basic idea—unconventional then—was that hard work (rather than social status or piety) was the key to virtue, and that human beings could always better themselves if they worked hard enough at the right things.

But what were the right things? Franklin had a general idea of the virtues involved in what he called "moral perfection." The problem was that he did not have a framework to follow—no clear delineation of the virtues, no rank order of them, no sequence for attending to them. He just tried to be good in all ways all at once and, as you might expect, soon ran into difficulty. "While my care was employed in guarding against one fault," he writes in his *Autobiography*, "I was often surprised by another; habit took the advantage of inattention; inclination was sometimes too strong for reason."[9]

Franklin decided a framework was necessary. Based on his extensive readings, he synthesized and compiled a list of thirteen main virtues, then considered how to go about improving himself in their regard. "I judged it would be well not to distract my attention by attempting the whole at once," Franklin wrote, "but to fix it on one of them at a time; and, when I should be master of that, then to proceed to another, and so on, till I should have gone thro' the thirteen; and, as the previous acquisition of some might facilitate the acquisition of certain others, I arranged them with that view."[10] For the record, the virtues, in order, were temperance, silence, order, resolution, frugality, industry, sincerity, justice, moderation, cleanliness, tranquility, chastity, and humility.[11]

Franklin does not claim that his framework enabled him to attain moral perfection, but it certainly aided him in trying.

PRACTICES

The creation of Franklin's framework brings us to practices, the how-to. This is one element that distinguishes the idea entrepreneur from other idea-driven figures: the ability to express an idea in behaviors and practices. In addition to the narrative and the conceptual framework, people are hungry for guidance about *how* to bring an idea into the fabric of everyday life. For many idea entrepreneurs, the gathering of practices starts very early in the process of accumulation, well before an idea begins to form.

Mireille Guiliano, for example, translates the French lifestyle into a number of simple behaviors: drink lots of water (and also drink more, although not too much more, champagne), walk whenever you can (climb the stairs even if you have an elevator), turn off the television. Cesar Millan urges us to start by understanding why dogs do what they do and then suggests how to respond. For example, dogs jump up because they want to assert dominance over you: don't encourage this behavior by acting affectionately in response. Millan picked up these behaviors as a boy on his grandfather's farm. The complete and defined set of practices that Millan contends will bring about good dog-human relationships developed over time.

Even psychologist and Nobel Prize winner Daniel Kahneman, who has long been associated with the world of academia, showed signs of wanting to reach a wider public and become an idea entrepreneur with the publication of *Thinking, Fast and Slow* (Farrar, Straus and Giroux, 2011) which is replete with insights and tips about how we think and how we can avoid mental mistakes. He coauthored an article in *Harvard Business Review* called "Before You Make That Big Decision . . . ," which shows how to apply some of his ideas to business decision making.[12] And he has cofounded a for-profit consulting firm, the Greatest Good, which has the goal of "applying rigorous, cutting-edge data analysis and economic methods to the most salient problems in business."[13]

How-to First

The practical and the theoretical, the tangible and the abstract, have a complementary effect—each informing the other.

It was by alternating his focus on theory and practice that Bryant Terry, a nutrition researcher, "eco-chef," and idea entrepreneur in the making, gradually came to his idea—that nutrition is key to social justice, particularly for young people of color.

Terry is the coauthor, with Anna Lappé, of *Grub: Ideas for an Urban Organic Kitchen*, (Tarcher/Penguin, 2006), which argues that urban living can be compatible with healthy, environmentally aware eating. The cookbook achieved widespread popularity and began a minor food movement whose distinctive expression was the "Grub Party," a potluck meal featuring Terry's eco-healthy-hip cuisine served in an urban community setting. His next book, *Vegan Soul Kitchen: Fresh, Healthy, and Creative African-American Cuisine* (Da Capo Press, 2009) in which he offers vegan versions of traditional African-American recipes, put him on the path of idea entrepreneurship.

Early Models

Terry's fascination with food started early. He was born in Memphis, Tennessee, in 1974 and raised in a large, extended family. Both sets of grandparents cultivated vegetable gardens, used the harvest to make meals for their families, and produced enough to give to their neighbors and share with members of their church. It wasn't hip or urban, but it was healthy and community based.

When he was a teenager, Terry had one of those iconic moments that revealed his particular food fascination. One day he heard the song "Beef," by hip-hop artist KRS-One. The song is about the process by which a cow is transformed from a living creature into plate-ready portions. KRS-One sings of the greed, speed, drugs, and stress involved.[14]

The song had a powerful effect on Terry and he asked his father for money to buy the album. His father agreed on one condition: that Bryant also had to check out a book from the local library; he suggested *The Jungle*, by Upton Sinclair, the classic exposé of the U.S. meatpacking industry, published in 1906. At the library, Terry fell into conversation with the librarian, who, as it turned out, was a vegan. "It was just one of those planets-aligning, beautiful moments in the universe," Terry said in a 2010 lecture at Yale University, which another member of our research team, Clara Silverstein, attended.[15]

Terry became a vegan and the librarian became a mentor. He quickly showed his proclivity for translating an idea into practices, although they were not particularly life-affirming at first. One day he grabbed a chicken that his mother had planned to cook for dinner and threw it in the garbage.

A Surprising Precedent

Terry set off on an academic path. He earned a BA in English from Xavier College in 1997, then moved to New York to work toward a PhD in American history at New York University.

While he was doing research into the black power movement of the 1960s and its relationship to the civil rights movement of the same period, Terry came across a surprising bit of information. He knew that the Black Panther Party had engaged in idea-driven action, some of it violent. And he knew that the Panthers also ran an initiative that involved giving away groceries and a Free Breakfast for Children Program. What he had not known was the extent of the Free Breakfast program's impact. It was, as he put it in his Yale presentation, a "brilliant, keen analysis about the intersection of malnutrition and poverty, and then doing something about it."[16]

Perhaps he could do something similar? At that time, Terry had gotten involved in a number of community-based social justice programs. As he thought about the Breakfast for Children Program, and about his fascination with veganism, he realized that people in the communities in which he was working had high rates of diet-related illnesses—such as "diabetes, heart disease, certain cancers," he said. The nexus of illness, income, and food availability (or lack of same) suddenly became clear to him. "How can we possibly expect people living in low-income, historically excluded communities to live long, healthy, sustainable lives when they don't even have real food available to them?"[17]

Terry saw that a purely academic approach, such as an after-school classroom-based program, would not attract the kids he wanted to connect with. Nor was he interested in the dogmatic approach he had tried on his mother and her chicken.

He decided that cooking would work. He would engage young people "in a way that was practical, that was fun, giving them tools that they could use in their adulthood."[18]

To put this practical plan into effect, however, Terry needed a bit more of a framework, an overarching theory. He decided that an act of leaving was required: he would have to step off the academic path, abandon the PhD plan, and devote his efforts into changing the thinking and behavior of inner-city kids. He left NYU (with a master's degree) and enrolled in the Natural Gourmet Institute's Chef's Training program.

In 2002, after earning his chef's diploma, Terry set to work on the how-to. He founded a program called b-healthy!—Build Healthy Eating and Lifestyles to Help Youth. The plan was to teach young people how to cook, how to incorporate more plant-based foods in their meals, and, just as important, how to translate this thinking into the practices of others in the community, such as food retailers. At first, his students were dubious. Vegetables, they explained to him, were "nasty."[19] But gradually, through a combination of talking and cooking and eating, the students came around to the pleasures of bananas and leafy greens.

Through this work, Terry teamed up with Anna Lappé—a food activist whose mother is Frances Moore Lappé, author of *Diet for a Small Planet*—to coauthor *Grub*, which was awarded a 2007 Nautilus Award for Social Change. The success of that book led Terry to other forms of expression, including a blog; a public television series, *The Endless Feast*; and, at last, his second book, *Vegan Soul Kitchen*. In it, Terry offers traditional African-American recipes rendered into the language and ingredients of veganism—such as Black-Eyed Pea Fritters and Upper Caribbean Creamy Grits with Roasted Plantain Pieces. The respiration around his book and his other projects launched a hectic round of speaking engagements, media interviews, and cooking demonstrations. In 2009 alone, he appeared at eighty events, which frequently took him far from his home base of Oakland, California.

His sacred expression, however, is to be found in his practices of food distribution and purchase and, of course, in that most fundamental and universal of practices: cooking.

PREPONDERANCE

The would-be idea entrepreneur often asks how *much* material—how many fragments of fascination, nuggets of content, frameworks, stories, and practices—is necessary to contemplate creating a more substantial expression and going public in a concerted way.

The answer is a preponderance—an abundance, a great heaviness of material. My friend and colleague George Stalk, a strategy expert and author of many books, says that you know you have a preponderance if you can pass the one-day test. That is, if you can talk about your idea for an entire day to an audience of smart people—and keep their interest and attention—you probably have enough material to go public.

For proof of the validity of this test, we can look to Edward Tufte, who has been presenting his material in the form of a one-day course, called Presenting Data and Information, since 1992.

Tufte is one of the seminal figures in the development of modern information graphics. The *New York Times* has called him the "da Vinci of data"[20] and *Business Week*, not to be out-alliterated, dubbed him the "Galileo of graphics."[21] Tufte is the creator of several books, the first and best known of which is *The Visual Display of Quantitative Information* (Graphics Press, 1983), which have, by his estimate, together sold more than 1.5 million copies as of 2009.[22]

In addition to his one-day course, Tufte also lectures and participates in forums, takes on some consulting engagements and advisory roles, offers a few items of merchandise for sale, and maintains an active website. He is also a fine artist and sculptor, with a gallery in Manhattan.

Tufte's idea is complex and nuanced: that visual design should make it more possible for people to engage with data and to find within it some larger meaning, causality or comparison, or something beyond just a collection of interesting numbers. As Tufte puts it: "Good design is clear thinking made visible."[23]

Tufte is driven by a long-held fascination—he was always, he writes, "enchanted by the elegant and precise beauty of the best displays of information."[24] He had a long accumulation period, much of it spent in academia. He earned a BA and MS in statistics from Stanford, then a PhD in political science from Yale. His two interests—data and political science—seemed to run in parallel for a time, and starting in 1967, he taught a course in political economy and data analysis at Princeton's Woodrow Wilson School of Public and International Affairs. He also wrote three books about political science, which were heavy on data.

It was not until the early 1980s that Tufte's material had achieved the status of a preponderance and that he decided to go public with a book very different from the ones he had written before: it would not only express his ideas about design, it would manifest them. Tufte doubted, however, that an academic publisher could produce a book as elegantly and precisely as he would require, so he decided to publish it himself. To do so, Tufte remortgaged his house (at an 18 percent interest rate), used the money to found his own publishing concern, the Graphics Press, and produced *The Visual Display of Quantitative Information*, a large, beautifully designed and printed work.[25] This became the iconic moment of going public for Tufte and the book his first major expression, replete with ideas, examples, analysis, lexicon, and a framework.

Tufte's one-day course, which I and other members of my team have attended, offers much but not all of his preponderance of material—in spoken form, along with visuals, but not the endless march of PowerPoint slides that Tufte deplores—and passes the Stalk test of accumulation with flying colors. Tufte speaks more or less nonstop for almost six hours. He is obviously fascinated with his topic and covers a lot of territory, including the following (as listed on his website): "fundamental strategies of analytical design"; "statistical data: tables, graphics and semi-graphics"; "multi-media, internet, and websites"; the "use of PowerPoint, video, overheads, and handouts"; and many other topics, all illustrated and explained with "many practical examples."[26]

So, to answer the question, "Do I have enough material to create a definitive expression, to go public?" If you can present for six hours, keep your audience engaged, and do so for twenty years, you're ready.

NECESSARY INGREDIENTS

Sometimes, however, the answer to the question is, and should be, *not really*.

The process of engaging with and revealing a fascination, accumulating material, and gradually shaping an idea can be burdensome, elusive, and just not for everybody. I count those people wise who consider going public but ultimately decide against it, when one or more of the elements—fascination, framework, practices—just aren't there.

As illustration, let me tell a brief story. A few years ago a literary agent, whom I love and respect, called me. He had a client whom he loved and respected. She had a "strong platform," as he put it, wanted to write a "big book," go public, break out, become an idea entrepreneur, achieve influence. The whole enchilada. (He may not have used that exact phrase.) Heather (not her real name) was a journalist and television personality, with a specialty in personal finance and her own show. She had published more than one book already, although none had gained much response. She had accumulated, the agent believed, a good deal of material. She had the educational credentials and the experiential chops.

Would I be interested in talking with her and helping her with a book?

Motive

Heather and I met in the Grill Room at the Harvard Club in New York, in the shadow of the stuffed big-game heads.

I asked her my usual questions.

"What is driving you to do this book?"

"It seems like the right time. Everybody is telling me I should."

"Ah. What particularly fascinates you about the topic?"

"Oh, it's all interesting to me. But nothing in particular, I guess."

"Well, you must have some good stories gathered from all that reporting?"

"Oh yes." I think she told me a couple but, whatever they were, I can't remember them now.

"What would you say is the fundamental human concern you want to connect with? How do you want to help people?"

"Managing money. People do it badly."

You may find this odd. By the time a would-be entrepreneur contemplates creating a major expression and going public, shouldn't the fascination have revealed itself? Shouldn't that wonderful con-tangulation of material have grown to such a preponderance that it is demanding to be deployed somehow, even if it doesn't yet fill up a day's worth of talking? Shouldn't the idea-sentence already have been articulated, many times over, even if imperfectly, and gotten some kind of positive response?

Yes. But then again, that's what the messy front end is all about. Sometimes people have a deep belief that they have something important to say and an urge to go public with it, but that's about as far as they have gone. Besides, that's my role. I don't usually get called in by those who have nailed their fascination, perfectly articulated their idea, are already brilliant at expression, and have a plan for breaking out.

At the end of our hour together, Heather and I were no closer to an idea, let alone a book, than when we started. I wasn't sure she wanted to proceed. I wasn't convinced there was anything to proceed with. Still, we agreed that we would both think some more and talk again in a week or two.

Weeks turned into months.

It was back-of-the-mind work, rather than constant heavy lift-ing. I reviewed her material, which I determined would not pass the one-day preponderance test. When I thought I had an approach that might work, or an idea that might fit her interests, I would be in touch with Heather and run it by her. She would listen care-fully. She would think about it for a couple of days. Then, in the nicest possible way, would say something like, "I don't know. It doesn't seem quite right."

At last the process came to an end. I told her that I didn't think I could help her. She agreed that we hadn't done what had to be done. We parted company on good terms. She said she would think some more. Gather some more material. Maybe revisit the project later.

Will

What happened? Was I missing something? Had my front-end chaos-navigation skills failed me and her? Or was Heather or her material missing something? I thought about that a good deal.

I came to the conclusion (based on the evaluation of many experiences, not just the one with Heather) that there is only one ingredient the idea entrepreneur must have and that Heather, indeed, did not have—at least not at that time.

That ingredient is will. Idea entrepreneurs must have the motivation and the drive to reveal themselves, gather a ton of material together, think it all through, express it in a serious and compelling way, go public with it, and try to break out from that glut that clogs the ideaplex.

All the other elements can be discovered, accumulated, developed, or articulated—although it may take time and a lot of work to do so. (Many a would-be idea entrepreneur who makes plans to go public within a year hence is still in the accumulation process a decade later.)

The will to break out is essential, but that does not mean it has to come before everything else. Very often, the will does not really strengthen and propel the idea entrepreneur into action until one of the other elements fuels it. The accumulation may provide a sense of confidence that the idea entrepreneur has more and richer material than anyone else has gone public with; this seems to have been true of Tufte. An expression may be so well received that it encourages the idea entrepreneur to try for more, as the publication of *Grub* did for Bryant Terry. It may be the persistent urging of friends and colleagues (Guiliano) or the admiration of a member of the ideaplex (Millan).

However and whenever it evidences itself, every idea entrepreneur eventually has—and in this way they are similar to the business-building entrepreneur—a powerful, driving, resilient will to animate their idea and infect the world with it.

THE PERSONAL NARRATIVE

Let me boil all that we have discussed in this chapter into a single endeavor, a never-ending activity of the idea entrepreneur: to create, shape, express, refine, and constantly live the *personal narrative*.

The personal narrative, for our purposes, is not the same as the relation of one's life history or the recitation of the highlights that make up one's resume. Nor is it a story in the sense that it has an arc of action, driven by character conflicts, that emerges from an initiating situation and arrives at a no-loose-ends denouement. Nor is it a fable or parable, a story designed to make a point or draw a lesson.

The personal narrative of the idea entrepreneur is the story of the creation of the idea. It weaves together two threads. One: the human conditions, phases, situations, actions, behaviors, and events of the idea entrepreneur's life. Two: the revelations, insights, learnings, syntheses, transformations, and understandings that have emerged during that life. The result is a narrative that is both human and hypothetical, concrete and abstract, emotional and intellectual.

The personal narrative takes time to live, effort to develop, skill to express, and some courage to take public. That is the work of the idea entrepreneur.

On the Train

One of the best examples of how life events intertwine with idea fragments to form a personal narrative concerns Mohandas Gandhi, another prototypical idea entrepreneur.

A brief bit of context. Gandhi was born in 1869 in India when the country was under British rule. He trained as a lawyer in England, passed the bar there in 1891, and returned to India to begin his career. He couldn't find a position that suited him, but in 1893 was offered work on a case in South Africa by a partner in an Indian firm that did business there. After much deliberation, Gandhi decided to go, expecting the work would keep him in Africa for a year or so at most. (He ended up staying, on and off, for more than twenty years.)

In April of that year, at age twenty-three, Gandhi traveled from India to Durban, a city on the east coast of South Africa, where the law firm had its offices. A few days later, he had to travel to Charlestown in the state of Pretoria to prepare for a case, and purchased a first-class ticket for the overnight train journey. He settled into his compartment and was alone there until the train stopped at Maritzburg, a station along the way, and another first-class passenger came aboard. The new passenger "looked me up and down," Gandhi writes in his *Autobiography*. "He saw that I was a 'coloured' man. This disturbed him."

The passenger fetched the railway officials, who told Gandhi that he would have to move to a lesser accommodation. Gandhi objected. "But I have a first-class ticket," he said. The officials didn't care. Gandhi held firm. Constables were called. At last Gandhi and his gear were removed from the train and he sat in the waiting room at Maritzburg, shivering in the cold and unable to read in the dark.

As he sat in the nighttime gloom of the Maritzburg waiting room, Gandhi thought hard about what had happened to him. He moved beyond the anger and the shame and the inconvenience and then, he writes, "I began to think of my duty. Should I fight for my rights or go back to India?" He concluded that he should "try, if possible, to root out the disease and suffer hardships in the process."[27]

From that moment forward, or so we believe from what he writes, Gandhi's personal fascination with race and caste, and his frustration with the treatment he had to suffer because of his being "coloured," became connected with his idea of social equality, his practice of nonviolent resistance, and, ultimately, his desire to put an end to the British Raj and to found an Indian nation.

In the train story, Gandhi becomes the idea, the idea becomes Gandhi. The meaning and import of such iconic moments are usually not so clear or brazen in the living of them. That's why the idea entrepreneur must look for these moments, clear away extraneous detail, determine their meaning, remember the emotions involved, and construct or reconstruct the train of thought.

A personal narrative of this sort can be quite short. Most of us will have only a few such intertwining moments. In Gandhi's autobiography, which is of considerable length, only a handful of moments qualify. If you can come up with two or three, you likely have the main elements of the personal narrative.

Deciding

One of those essential intertwinings, interestingly enough, is likely to be when you decide it is time to create an important expression, to go public, to try to break out. The method and motive of doing so becomes an important part of the narrative.

Mireille Guiliano, for example, did not decide to go public until she could fit that piece of the narrative with the rest of her life story. When that happened, she had already built a long and successful career as an executive—and ultimately the CEO—of Clicquot, Inc., the champagne maker. During her twenty years with Clicquot, one of her management duties was to act as a spokesperson for champagne and unofficial ambassador for the French lifestyle. In this capacity, she traveled throughout the United States, delivering lectures and giving talks on a variety of food- and lifestyle-related topics: The history of champagne. The French lifestyle. Gastronomy.

Not only did Guiliano have to learn a great deal to make her presentations, she also gained knowledge from others—and gathered their stories—during the talks, but especially during the meals and get-togethers that followed, which always featured good food and nice wines. She was accumulating.

At those events, people invariably came up to Guiliano at the end of the evening. "You're so passionate about food and wine," they would say. "We read about you in magazines. You say you like to cook and you entertain a lot." Inevitably came the question: *How come you're not fat?*

Guiliano would smile and reply, "Well, French women don't get fat."

"So you should write a book about that," people would say.

But Guiliano was not interested or, at least, could not find a rationale for writing a book that made sense to her. She was content with her life and did not have any great motivation to go public. Still, she could not help pondering the questions that came her way. Why, indeed, did she not get fat? And what was it that these women thought that she, Mireille, had to offer them? It had to do with lifestyle, and *joie de vivre*, for sure.

As time went along, Guiliano heard the same question, over and over, not only from people at her professional engagements but also from her friends. They wondered how it was that—even with all that travel and all those restaurant meals—she never seemed to overindulge, never put on extra pounds, and, what's more, always seemed upbeat about her life. Her approach to food and eating seemed so different from that of her friends in New York and around the country, women who seemed to have unhappy relationships with eating and with their bodies.

"I'd go out to restaurants and they were always guilty about food: 'I can't have dessert. I can't have that—it's sinful.' I was shocked," Guiliano told Anna and me. When she traveled back to France, she was particularly struck by the differences, which only seemed to get more pronounced as the years went by. "I'd get together with friends there and they would plan great meals." Eating in France was fun, convivial, angst-free, and, oddly enough, did not seem to lead to weight gain as it did with American women. (Of course, there are fat women in France and their numbers are increasing, as they are worldwide, but that doesn't negate Guiliano's message.)

Watching her friends and thinking about the issue, Guiliano's iconic moments as a teenager in Weston came back to her. She realized that her personal fascination was deeply relevant to the problems of her American friends. "I remembered how miserable I was when I struggled with my weight," she said. "I was seeing my American friends in pain. So I started helping them." Informally, one on one, she began sharing the ideas and practices that she had lived, interpreted, and experimented with since she was a young woman in France.

She saw that what she had to offer was genuinely helpful to others. She realized that she had tucked away a great deal of knowledge and information, observations and stories, a kind of framework. She had always had the vague notion that, eventually, she would do *something* with all of that stuff. And, even as a college student, she had thought about writing something, someday, although she wasn't sure what or how.

But Guiliano's mother had always admonished her never to put herself forward, never to put herself ahead of others. Besides, Guiliano genuinely had no desire for fame and money was not a driver, nor did she really think of herself as a writer, one who cannot live without the craft. So she had put the idea of writing a book "in a little box" in the back of her mind, as she called it, and it remained in a "little corner" for years.

A Perspective

It was a friend who offered Guiliano the perspective that enabled her to take the public step. The friend had been prodding her for years to write a book. Guiliano had always smiled but said no, over and over again. Finally, however, her friend tried a different approach. She argued that it would not be about the writing, the effort would be about *helping people*.

Helping people; that was different. That was in Guiliano's DNA. It made sense as a motive. It was one of her family's values, one of her mother's teachings. Helping people with ideas and practices would be very different from aggrandizing oneself with a book.

Guiliano decided the time had come to express herself.

3

EXPRESSION

An idea is not really an idea until it is expressed—and expressed in the fullest, most powerful, and most compelling form you can create.

All of the elements we've talked about so far—the fascination, revelations, iconic moments, the accumulation of material, the nascent framework, the practices, the miscellaneous expressions—are stored inside that little box in your mind, as well as whatever physical or electronic containers you maintain. As you consider and synthesize all of that, you gradually come to think it has cohered—or soon could be made to cohere—into a body of material and an idea with which you could *go public*.

Going public is the time when you decide to make a serious, deliberate move to take the idea to a new level. Rather than think about it as an interest or a sideline, the furtherance of the idea will become your primary effort—all other activities will be secondary.

(This is why idea entrepreneurs, in their books and from the lectern, profusely thank the families they have seen so little of for the preceding two or three years.) You become willing to separate yourself from current thinking and conventional behavior—and perhaps leave behind current roles or professional paths—that are contrary to the idea or get in the way of pursuing it. You commit whatever resources of time, energy, goodwill, and money you can to create an expression of greater scope or clearer purpose than any you have created before. You set out to distinguish yourself from other idea entrepreneurs and expressions that are already out there.

The precise reason for going public at a particular moment is often difficult to discern and may always remain a mystery, but there are three general drivers. First, idea entrepreneurs tend to have healthy egos and, when they feel they have sufficient accumulation of material, have demonstrated their superior knowledge on their topic—and often, feel frustrated and dissatisfied with the current state of thinking—something clicks and they're ready to step out.

The second driver is the lure of the ideaplex. Many would-be idea entrepreneurs indulge in what I call fantasy #1, which goes something like this: My book will be published and instantly appear on the *New York Times* best-seller list. Oprah will want me to come on her show and I will charm her. I will deliver a killer TED talk. The video version will go viral. I could win an Academy Award. (The last part usually makes no sense, but it is, after all, a fantasy.)

Finally and perhaps most important, the idea entrepreneur is driven by the desire to do good and help others. You think about what other people—those who are out there in your as-yet-undefined audience—need and want from you and your idea, about what contribution you can make to the world, rather than what your idea can bring to you in terms of personal satisfaction or a boost in reputation.

The idea entrepreneurs who remain on the stage the longest usually keep their ego in check, get over the fantasy (or never fall prey to it), and come to the realization that the desire to do good for others will bring them the greatest influence in the long run. Zig Ziglar, an expert in sales, author of several books, and a motivational speaker for some forty years (doing as many as 150 engagements per year at $50,000 each), put it well. "Our whole philosophy's built around the concept that you can have everything in life you want if you will just help enough other people get what they want."[1]

Going public does not imply that you have thus far spent your time in a cave, with no expression of your idea. Tufte had written three books before he made the big push with *Visual Display of Quantitative Information* and his one-day course. Guiliano had been speaking and participating in events around the country for years before she took the plunge with her book. Millan had been working with packs-full of dogs before he was ready to be the center of a television show called *The Dog Whisperer*.

The act of going public is always precipitated or enabled by an expression—usually the sacred expression—that breaks out from everything the idea entrepreneur has done before and also from the glut of ideas that are already in the same idea space.

Expression is, therefore, a double-duty process by which an idea is both more fully formulated—beyond the state of contangulation—*and* delivered to others.

INFECTING

On the subject of expression, let me offer the thoughts of Leo Tolstoy (1828–1910). As the reader is no doubt more than aware, Tolstoy was the author of two great novels—*War and Peace* and

Anna Karenina—but he was also an essayist. In his 1897 work, *What Is Art?*, Tolstoy offers a definition of art that is applicable to the idea entrepreneur's act of expression.

"Art is a human activity," Tolstoy writes, "consisting in this, that one man consciously, by means of certain external signs, hands on to others feelings he has lived through, and that other people are infected by these feelings, and also experience them."[2]

If we substitute the word *expression* for *art* (and mentally replace the word *man* with *person*), this is a useful and telling description of what the idea entrepreneur seeks to do.

Let me deconstruct the statement a bit. The word *consciously* is important, because it suggests that the artist/expresser is deliberately and intentionally embarking on the act of expression. This distinguishes it from another definition of art that Tolstoy, in the same essay, defines as "the manifestation of some mysterious Idea of beauty"—and which he put no stock in.[3] In other words, the idea entrepreneur makes a deliberate decision to go public with a major expression; it does not mystically emerge.

Tolstoy goes on to say that this activity is about the handing on to others certain feelings that the artist/idea entrepreneur *has lived through*—not those he or she has heard about or observed or invented or borrowed from others. And, for our purposes, I think we can broaden the word *feelings* to include thoughts and ideas. I equate this with the "handing-on" of the personal narrative that is essential for the idea entrepreneur.

Although Tolstoy, as a writer, was partial to writing as his favored form of expression, he was generous in accepting that the handing-on of emotions could be accomplished through other modes of expression, too, including "movements, lines, colors, sounds, or forms expressed in words."[4] And, with that, he has pretty much covered the waterfront of the idea entrepreneur's available forms: writing, speaking, and, to a lesser degree, creating images or, as I call them, emblems.

The key phrase now arrives. Tolstoy says the purpose of this activity of art (expression, for us) is to hand on these feelings such that others are "infected" by them. (Although I have also seen the Russian translated as "affected.") Shades of virality! Ideas as a kind of virus (think of Seth Godin and the "idea virus" and Everett Rogers's "diffusion of innovations"), a contagion that spreads among groups in more or less predictable ways.

There's one more important piece of Tolstoy's statement to be considered, and then we'll return him to the shelf. Not only are others infected by the words or movements, *they also experience the feelings for themselves.* This is precisely what the idea entrepreneur would like as a response to his or her expressions: for others to experience the revelations and iconic moments such that they become embedded in their minds. Tolstoy continues, noting that when this handing-on, infecting, and experiencing takes place, art/expression operates as "a means of union among [people], joining them together in the same feelings." And finally, says Tolstoy, it is "indispensable for the life and progress toward well-being of individuals and of humanity."[5]

Life affirmation. Improvement. Making a difference. The starting of movements. Changing the world.

Sacred Articulation

As I've said, it is likely that the nascent idea entrepreneur has expressed (or tried to express) the idea, or at least parts of it, many times and in many forms during the period of accumulation.

The expression that enables a person to go public, however, may indeed emerge with a different kind of energy than all the others that came before and, usually, all those that follow. Most often, but not always, this going-public expression is the one that comes to be seen as the idea entrepreneur's sacred expression. I use the term just a bit facetiously, but it is apt, because this expression is the one in which, for the first time, the idea is clearly and completely articulated and the personal narrative is openly related and connected to the idea. This expression is the definitive version, the original source, the final authority. To paraphrase and differently apply the thoughts of Victorian art critic John Ruskin (1819–1900), the sacred expression is the one that contains the greatest number of the idea entrepreneur's greatest ideas.[6]

Writing, particularly the writing of a book, has long been the most common form of sacred expression for the idea entrepreneur, but today the book is just one of many forms. The fifteen- to eighteen-minute TED talk, or its equivalent in other eduinfotainment venues, has become a common form of sacred expression for the idea entrepreneur and other forms—including the video, the blog, and an extended Twitter presence (which is a favored form in China)—can play that role, as well.

Still, the book continues to be an important expression for the idea entrepreneur, even when it is not the sacred one, for a number of reasons. The most obvious is that writing a book forces you to think more comprehensively, holistically, and rigorously about the idea than does any other form of expression. A friend recently suggested to me that many ideas are better expressed and comprehended in a shorter form of writing, such as an article—in print or online. "I can get the entire idea, at least as much as I need of it, in a good piece in the *Harvard Business Review*," he said. "Too many books are just puffed-up articles."

I have heard this argument many times and I don't disagree. However, it may be more accurate to think of the best idea-driven articles—the ones that present a strong narrative, clear framework, and useful set of practices—as un-puffed books. They are condensations or summaries of a book-length piece of writing and are so powerful and clear precisely because the rigorous thinking has been accomplished in the act of creating a book.

So, even when the idea entrepreneur has had some success with public speaking and special events, appearing in videos, or writing blogs and tweeting, he usually approaches a book project with trepidation and wariness. I have seen this many times: the confident, successful, sometimes headstrong person who has achieved influence and even fame as a content expert who, when facing the task of writing a book, wilts a little.

STARTING AT THE TOP

Mireille Guiliano is hardly a wilter, as far as I can tell, but it still took a lot for her—even beyond the urging of her friends and the discovery of a suitable motivation (helping others)—to decide to go public with her idea. Once the decision was made, however, she aimed high and was clear about her ambitions: she wanted the book to be a best-seller.

To that end, she knew she needed a top-notch publisher and, to get a good publisher, she needed to secure a reputable agent. In the spring of 2003, she prepared a book proposal and, through personal connections, got it to a literary agent, Kathy Robbins at the Robbins Office, in New York.

For all of you who have tried to sell a book with a proposal, this next part of the story may be difficult to hear. Not only did Robbins agree to represent Guiliano, she declared that she would not mess around with a general submission to multiple publishers, as is customary, but would take it straight to the publisher that she considered the very best for Guiliano's book, Alfred A. Knopf, one of the legends of the publishing industry. To make a short story shorter, Knopf bought the book almost immediately and three weeks later, Guiliano had a contract. The manuscript would be due in six months. That was that.

Oh yes, she did still have to write the thing. And in this matter, Guiliano did not immediately make a commitment to put the creation of her expression above all other activities. She was, after all, a globe-trotting executive, the steward of a legendary brand, Veuve Clicquot, and leader of a large company, Clicquot, Inc. She had position, income, security, networks, a reputation. She figured she would be able to continue in her position and also write a book.

But once she really faced up to the task, Guiliano began to wonder if she *could* manage both a book and a corporation. And, even with an instant contract and support from her agent, she found that the confidence that had propelled her through the selling of the proposal flagged a bit when it came to the actual writing. "I didn't think I had that talent," Guiliano told Anna and me. "I'm not a writer. It's not my profession."

Most idea entrepreneurs do not start out dreaming of becoming writers, at least not in the way that other writers, especially those of fiction, do. They may find no particular joy or sustenance or fulfillment in the act and craft of writing itself and, in fact, it may be very hard work for them, something to be avoided. So, when the moment arrives, they sometimes wonder if this is really the right way to go public.

Panic Time

Mild panic set in. It didn't take long for Guiliano to conclude that her assumption had been wrong. To get the book done on time, she would have to quit her job, after all. Her husband, Edward, supported her decision, but the company chairman, based in Paris, had other ideas. He saw the book as a great opportunity to promote the Clicquot brand. He asked how many copies Guiliano thought she could sell.

"Two hundred thousand," Guiliano answered, without blinking an eye. They both knew that was a big number. Guiliano had author friends whose books sold only a few thousand copies at best. But she held firm. "I would not have decided to write the book if I thought it would sell so little," she told us.

The chairman liked the sound of two hundred thousand books out there whose author had such a close connection with the Clicquot brand. He was smart and persuasive in his efforts to keep her with the company. *Take the time you need to write. Delegate more.* At last, Guiliano agreed. For weeks, she tried to write at the office. It was impossible. She wrote bits and pieces, but essentially got nowhere. Even so, she did not quit her position.

When summer came, and still the pages had not filled as she had wished, Guiliano knew she had to take a different tack. At the rate of zero words per day, she would finish the book approximately never. She had to step up the effort. She had to put the book first. She and Edward had planned a two-week vacation to Sardinia and she decided she would have to use that time to write. They agreed they would have breakfast together, Edward would disappear until one, and then they would have "the afternoon to play together," Guiliano said. In the evening she would return to work, devoting another four hours to editing the morning's pages and preparing for the next day's writing.

It worked. By the third day of writing, the words were pouring out. By the end of the seventh day she had written enough material that, combined with the bits and pieces she had already composed, she had almost half the book in hand. By the time they left Sardinia, two weeks later, the book was well on its way to completion. She polished it off in the evenings and on weekends that fall. By Christmas 2003 it was done, all four hundred pages of it. The editors at Knopf laughed. They were preparing Bill Clinton's autobiography at the time, which came in at 957 pages. "We love your prose, but you're not Clinton," they said. They cut the book to half its original length. (Not to worry, Guiliano's agent told her; the remaining material is almost enough to fill book #2.)

Anticipating

Then Guiliano had to endure the wilderness that stretches between the day the final manuscript is submitted and the time the book hits the market—which, in her case, was almost exactly a year. She continued with her work at Clicquot, not knowing how the book might fare or what success would mean for her, or if indeed she could sell two hundred thousand copies.

For those of you who have published books and watched as the ideaplex ignored or toyed with them, this next part may also be a little irritating. *French Women Don't Get Fat* was published in December 2004, and the ideaplex embraced it. The book was reviewed or featured in general interest media, business journals, and specialty publications including *Newsweek, People*, the *San Francisco Chronicle, BusinessWeek*, and *Town & Country*. The take on it was positive. Janet Maslin, in the *New York Times*, wrote: "Ms. Guiliano turns out to be eminently level headed. She combines reasonable thoughts about nutrition with a general endorsement of joie de vivre, and her tone is girl friendly enough to account for the book's runaway popularity."[7]

French Women Don't Get Fat became a best-seller and not just in the United States, but also internationally—it was translated into thirty-nine languages. Requests for interviews and speaking dates came flooding in. The publisher arranged a promotional tour with stops all over the country and then outside the United States. At last, it became clear that Guiliano had to make a choice. She could not be a full-time executive, globe-trotting author, and an attentive spouse. Something had to give. In early February of 2005,

Guiliano was in San Francisco, without Edward, to do a series of interviews, after which she was headed for Australia to do more of the same, still without her husband. The two had never been apart on Valentine's Day. They talked it over and Edward agreed to meet her in Australia.

On Valentine's Day, Guiliano did the whirl of book promotions and interviews from morning until evening. She got back to the hotel room with just enough time to wish Edward good night, but revealed with dismay that she would not be joining him in bed. She had a conference call to make, for business, at 3 a.m. Australian time. With Edward asleep in the next room, Guiliano was on the phone for an hour, all the while thinking, *This is not good. This is not good.* By the time she hung up, she had decided to resign. She left her CEO position at the end of 2005, putting herself on the path to becoming an idea entrepreneur.

PULLED IN

Not everyone deliberately chooses to go public or, if they do, have as much control over, or success with, how the ideaplex responds. Mireille Guiliano bided her time and accepted a push to go public when the pushing finally felt right. For Hannah Salwen, however, the act of going public was essentially thrust upon her.

Hannah is the coauthor, with her father Kevin Salwen, of *The Power of Half: One Family's Decision to Stop Taking and Start Giving Back* (Houghton Mifflin Harcourt, 2010), which tells the story of an audacious idea, a family project that proposed a practice that others could adapt and follow.

It involved philanthropy and the family home. At Hannah's urging (she was then fourteen years old), the Salwens—much to the amazement of the world, as well as to the shock and even chagrin of many of their friends and family—sold their mansion in Atlanta, the house where Hannah and her brother Joe had grown up, moved to a much smaller place, and donated half the proceeds from the sale (some $800,000) to charity—specifically to a philanthropic organization called the Hunger Project, which used the funds to establish community centers in Ghana.

Hannah's fundamental idea: most of us have so much more stuff than we need that we should give away much more of it than we do, even to the point of reducing our own circumstances.

Hannah talked about the project with Anna and me when we met with her in New York in the fall of 2011, soon after she had arrived to begin studies in an undergraduate nursing program at New York University, and a year and a half after *The Power of Half* came out.

When Salwen entered the NYU Torch Club, at first Anna wasn't sure it was her. Hannah looked quite different from the girl, the young woman, on the cover of the book, in the Google images. The most striking difference was simple: she had been a brunette and now she was blond. When her book *The Power of Half* came out, she was a high school sophomore, living in Atlanta, Georgia with her family. Now she was a college freshman—just one week into classes—at New York University in Washington Square. She had not told her new roommate about the book, the appearances on *Good Morning America*, any of that stuff. She did not want anybody to know. But her roommate had Googled her and found out.

When you interview someone who has been interviewed a hundred times before on the same subject, you are torn between wanting to hear the same old story from, as it were, the horse's mouth, and wanting to probe into new areas, uncover new secrets, gain startling insights. One always imagines that the interviewee will form a special bond with you and tell you the real story that all those other interviewers couldn't get.

Hannah Salwen seemed to understand that quite well. She talked openly and honestly about what she wanted to talk about, but also edited herself, steering away from topics she seemed to want to avoid. She was, in short, already a canny in the ways of the ideaplex.

Homeless Guys

Hannah's fascination first became evident in fifth grade when, as part of a school program connected to the curriculum on philanthropy, she volunteered at Café 458 in downtown Atlanta, a restaurant that donates some of its profits to help homeless people and also offers free meals to them on weekdays. At Café 458, Hannah took particular interest in a homeless man named Henry. He was just a "guy who used to always sit alone at this café," Hannah said. "I always used to feel so bad for him. I always wanted to sit with him. And I always just wanted to say, 'Henry, how is your day going?'" But she never did, although she often stopped by his table. "I remember the emotions that I felt when I would see him come in and order whatever he was ordering and sit alone and be really quiet."

The program was a revelation for Hannah. "School has never been my thing," she told us. "I kept telling my parents that all of the geniuses in the world failed out of school and it wouldn't be the end of the world if I failed out." This did not sit particularly well with her well-educated parents, even though they sympathized with her interest in doing good. Both Joan and Kevin Salwen had made giving back an important part of their lives, by getting involved in the United Way and Habitat for Humanity, among other activities. They even took in an entire family from New Orleans in the wake of Hurricane Katrina.

Hannah might have continued on with her local volunteering just as she had since fifth grade, had it not been for the iconic moment she experienced one early fall day in 2006. As father and daughter relate in the book and in their talks, Kevin was driving Hannah home from a sleepover and pulled their car to a stop at a red light about a mile from the house they would later sell. Hannah looked out the window. To the left, she saw a disheveled man hunched against a chain-link fence, holding a sign with the hand-lettered words "HUNGRY, HOMELESS, PLEASE HELP."[8] Hannah, whose family could be described as affluent to wealthy, had been working with the homeless for three years already and was used to such sights. Then Hannah looked to her right, as a black Mercedes pulled up beside them.

Nothing about either the homeless guy or the Mercedes driver was unusual, but the juxtaposition jolted Hannah. "Dad, if that man," she said, pointing to the Mercedes driver, "had a less nice car, that man there"—she gestured toward the homeless man—"could have a meal."

"Yeah. But you know, if *we* had a less nice car," Kevin replied, "he could have a meal."[9]

That was the revelatory moment, and it was the story that the ideaplex would later latch on to. The light turned green and the Salwens headed home, but Hannah could not get the image or put the thought out of her mind. That night, and again three nights later while the family ate Chinese takeout, she provoked a family conversation about affluence and giving back. Hannah thought the family should do more than they had been doing to help others, but her parents thought they were already doing a lot, what with the work with the United Way and Hannah's volunteering at Café 458.

Hannah persisted. *We can do more.* Finally, Joan, in an effort to test Hannah's resolve, said something to the effect of, "What do you want to do, sell our house?"[10] Hannah said, essentially, *yes.*

After much further discussion, the Salwens—against all the inclinations of a family brought up on the American dream that home ownership is good and bigger home ownership is better—decided to go for the plan.

They agreed to put the house on the market.

Tug

At first, the Salwens had no intention of going public with their idea. It was not one of those stunt projects cooked up for the express purpose of gaining attention from the ideaplex (e.g., *Living Oprah: My One-Year Experiment to Walk the Walk of the Queen of Talk* by Robyn Okrant or *The Year of Living Biblically: One Man's Humble Quest to Improve Himself by Living as a Woman, Becoming George Washington, Telling No Lies, and Other Radical Tests* by A. J. Jacobs). Although they didn't necessarily think of it this way, the act of selling the house—a practice, if a rather grand one—would be their sacred expression.

Not only did the Salwens have no plans for going public, they quickly learned that going public—even in a small way—could have its downsides. Not long after they settled on the plan, they told a few friends and family members about their intentions. Most thought the idea was crazy, upsetting, or absurd. From that moment on, the Salwens kept a low profile. Joan said she did not want to be made to feel like a "weirdo."[11]

Still, the house was on the market and the project played a big role in their lives, so the Salwens didn't try to hide what they were doing. Joan was a bit concerned, however, that Joe, Hannah's younger brother, wasn't as engaged in the project as she would have liked. Then she learned about a contest called My Home: The American Dream, sponsored by Coldwell Banker, the real estate company, and Scholastic, the publisher. Students were asked to share their own stories, in words and pictures, and describe how their dwellings "are not just structures in which they live, but homes where dreams are shared and memories are made."[12] Joe, with his father's help, made a video called *Hannah's Lunchbox*, sent it in, and won the top prize in his grade group.

This three-minute homemade video, which hadn't even been particularly hip or gone viral, started the process of going public. Kevin Salwen was a longtime member of the ideaplex, as a reporter and eventually a columnist at the *Wall Street Journal*, then as cofounder of a media company that published a short-lived magazine called *Motto*, which featured stories about business-people who also believed in the importance of doing social good.

In an e-mail exchange with a friend who was a producer at the *Today* show, Kevin included a link to Joe's video. The producer was intrigued and, soon thereafter, popped the question: would the Salwens like to appear on the *Today* show in a regular segment called "Making a Difference"?

Would they?

The Salwens debated the issue at length. Mother Joan was dead-set against the idea. The family had already taken enough grief about their project, and besides, they hadn't even sold the house yet; the story wasn't complete. Joe, however, was all for it. Hannah had no reservations either. She said, yes, of course, why wouldn't they go for it? Kevin argued that their appearance on the show could encourage others to do similar kinds of good, which seemed to bring Joan around.

They said yes. The taping took place that spring and it was fun, if a little contrived, as these things generally are. They shot scenes in New York, where Hannah gave a speech at the annual meeting of the Hunger Project, their chosen philanthropy. They also shot scenes in Atlanta: Hannah volunteering at Café 458, the family having breakfast together, Hannah touring the TV crew through the mansion (complete with antique elevator) at 116 Peachtree Circle, Hannah pointing out the intersection where the iconic moment had occurred.

The *Today* segment aired that summer. The piece was only a couple of minutes long, featuring reporter John Larson, and was positive, even laudatory. The show's hosts—Matt Lauer, Meredith Vieira, and Ann Curry—applauded the kids and the parents for their efforts. "A big kiss to that entire family!" said Curry. "Hannah, you rock!"[13]

The *Today* show piece generated a lot of attention for the Salwens and their project, but still, they could have carried on without any further adventures in the ideaplex. Then a friend suggested to Kevin that there might also be a book to be written about the Salwen family project. A television presence—even a single appearance on a major show—is attractive to publishers. If you have one expression that has gained a positive response, so the thinking goes, it might work in another form, too. (For example: Tina Fey and Lena Dunham, both of whom made their name in television, landed big book deals.)

Kevin, the journalist in the family, was most attracted by the idea. "Anyone want to write a book with me?" he asked everyone. Joan: no. Joe: no. Hannah: yes.

Then things happened fast, just as they had for Guiliano. The Salwens secured an agent who helped them put together a proposal and stir up enough interest from publishers to create an auction. The Salwens chose to publish with Houghton Mifflin Harcourt, which offered an advance against royalties of $380,000, a considerable sum for unknown first-time authors, even those who had appeared on the *Today* show.[14] Publication was targeted for a year hence.

Shove

The Power of Half was published in January 2010 and provoked glowing comment from influential members of the ideaplex.

Nicholas Kristof, the *New York Times* columnist who is known for his skepticism regarding do-gooders and their initiatives, wrote a piece called "What Could You Live Without?" He described the Salwen's endeavor as "crazy, impetuous and utterly inspiring."[15] Other pieces appeared in the *New Yorker* and *Parade* magazine—which ran an excerpt from the book with the title "Why We Gave Away Our House." Bill and Melinda Gates arranged for the Salwens to bring their message to Seattle.[16] In a segment on ABC News, host Diane Sawyer introduced the Salwen story with the question, "Would you give up half of everything you have because of a challenge from your child?"[17]

Never mind that the Salwens had neither given away half of "everything they had," as Diane Sawyer suggested, nor had they given away their house, as *Parade* put it. The Salwens had inarguably done something different, something good, something involving Africa, something heterodox: Who sells a beautiful house if they don't have to? In the midst of the 2008 bursting of the housing bubble and with home prices plummeting, the story offered a refreshing and inspiring twist.

Kevin and Hannah spent a good deal of their time in the ideaplex over the next eighteen months. They signed up with CAA, the Creative Artists Agency—a heavy hitter in the agency business, with clients including the likes of George Clooney and Peyton Manning—to represent them for speaking engagements. CAA did its job. By the time Hannah graduated from high school in the spring of 2011, she figured she had told her story in public 437 times, given 62 speeches in just one year at various venues and before all kinds of audiences around the country, and been interviewed 236 times for newspapers, magazines, TV shows, and radio stations. Not to mention all the blogs and tweets and conversations that she engaged in directly and that were exchanged about her without her participation.

Hannah became an—almost accidental—idea entrepreneur before she had even finished high school.

UP FROM NOWHERE

Not all idea entrepreneurs can or do think about going public in the rather grand way that Guiliano and Hannah Salwen did; instead, they are just focused on expressing their idea as best they can and making the expression available to those who might be interested in or helped by it. *If my friends and family like it, that would be enough.* Best-sellerdom, virality, and attention from the media do not really cross their mind, at least at first. But the current state of the ideaplex—which enables anyone to create a blog, self-publish and distribute a book, post a video, put oneself in a webcast, find some forum for a talk—makes it possible to go public, and in a big way, from a base of essentially nothing.

This is exactly what happened to Eckhart Tolle (pronounced TOLE-ee), who went from being a spiritual practitioner known only to a small circle of friends and colleagues to an internationally known teacher and leader who has been called "the most successful spiritual author of the modern age."[18] Tolle went public with the book that is now regarded as his sacred expression, *The Power of Now: A Guide to Spiritual Enlightenment*. It started out as a self-published, hand-distributed book with a few thousand copies in print, and became a massive best-seller with millions of copies in circulation around the world.

Of all the idea entrepreneurs in this book, Tolle is probably the one whose reach is the longest, influence the greatest, and model the most remarkable. And yet, it is important to note that I often mention Tolle's name or the title of his book to people of many different descriptions, and their reaction is: *Who?*

Wandering

Tolle followed a long, arduous, and pretty strange path of accumulation before he made the move to go public, but it had all the elements we expect of the idea entrepreneur, including iconic moments, revelations (of an especially intense variety), leavings, and a decision moment.

This is his story, as he tells it, with some details gleaned from other sources. (I did not interview Tolle.) His early life, at least in the way he relates it, does not display the clear moments of revelation that the lives of other idea entrepreneurs do. He was born as Ulrich, not Eckhart, Tolle in 1948 in the village of Lunen, Germany, not far from the border with the Netherlands. His parents fought and divorced, and Ulrich lived with his mother until he was thirteen, at which point he left school and went to live with his father in Spain. There he studied at home, reading widely, learning Spanish and several other languages, and delving into astronomy.[19]

Tolle moved to London at age nineteen, where he worked at a language school and then, in his twenties, matriculated at the University of London.[20] Intending to pursue the life of an academic, he went on to the University of Cambridge and began his graduate studies. He was bookish and withdrawn and thought of himself as a disappointment—his mother felt the same way. "My mother thought I'd failed miserably in life," said Tolle in an interview with Douglas Todd of the *Vancouver Sun*. "She was unhappy for many years."[21] Tolle lived, he writes in *The Power of Now*, "in a state of almost continuous anxiety interspersed with periods of suicidal depression."[22]

When Tolle did finally come to an iconic moment it was a blockbuster. He describes the experience in the introduction to *The Power of Now*. "One night not long after my twenty-ninth birthday," Tolle writes, "I woke up in the early hours with a feeling of absolute dread." He had had such episodes before, but never so intense. Everything around him seemed "alien" and "hostile" and "so utterly meaningless that it created in me a deep loathing of the world. The most loathsome thing of all, however, was my own existence."[23]

Tolle began to feel a "deep longing for annihilation, for nonexistence" and declared "I cannot live with myself any longer." This thought struck him deeply and he began to consider its meaning. "If I cannot live with myself, there must be two of me: the 'I' and the 'self' that 'I' cannot live with."[24]

This realization caused Tolle to feel, as he describes in the book, as if he were being pulled into a vortex, sucked toward a void. He felt fear; his body shook. Some time later, he became aware of the chirping of a bird. He found that he had lost all fear, all anxiety. The world seemed fresh and new. "For the next five months, I lived in a state of uninterrupted deep peace and bliss," he writes. He lived for some two years with none of the elements of a "socially defined identity." He had no home, no job; he claims to have had no relationships with other people, and spent much of his time "sitting on park benches in a state of the most intense joy."[25]

Tolle spent the next few years "probably living below the poverty line," with no savings, insurance, or investments, according to Todd's profile of Tolle.[26] Although there is very little confirmed information about this period, he seems to have slept on friends' couches, spent days in the parks of central London, and wandered through life.[27] Following regular visits to the library to read philosophy, Tolle concluded that what he had experienced was a form of enlightenment, and, accordingly, he changed his first name to Eckhart from Ulrich, in honor of German mystic Eckhart von Hochheim (1260–1327), commonly known as Meister Eckhart.[28] Tolle now often refers to himself as Meister Eckhart.

The Time Came

Slowly the new Eckhart Tolle began to emerge. He got into meditation, began to teach classes, and lived in Glastonbury—England's center of alternative lifestyles—for a time.

In 1994, at the age of forty-six, while Tolle was on a trip to America, the moment of decision arrived. In Sausalito, California, an "empowered energy stream" took hold of him. He felt compelled by an unnamed inner urge to express himself. He began to write.[29]

In 1996, while living in Vancouver and still working on what would become *The Power of Now,* Tolle made a connection with a management consultant named Connie Kellough, who was interested in engaging in a spiritual practice called a *sangha.* She asked Tolle to lead her and a small group in weekly sessions.

"Eckhart led us deeper and deeper into a state of stillness, in which we became increasingly attuned to the Presence at the heart of everything," Kellough writes on her website. "Eckhart not only exuded the energy of Presence, but he was also able to express perennial spiritual truths in an idiom suited to our times. His clear, contemporary language conveyed deep insights that enabled me to recognize him for the profound and timely teacher he is, especially for the West."[30]

After some months Kellough learned that Tolle was working on a book; eventually he approached her and asked, "Constance, would you consider being my publisher?" Kellough had no experience in publishing, but after some thought, she "began to see that behind the chronological storylines of Eckhart's life and [her] own ran a thread of spiritual intent that was the work of an invisible weaver."[31]

According to Kellough, she and Tolle worked together for months on the manuscript. It was completed in early 1997 and self-published under the imprint Namaste Press, which Kellough still runs. They had few resources available for marketing or distribution and, according to Kellough, often carried books into stores themselves, sometimes selling a few copies, sometimes not. Still, *The Power of Now* gradually began to gain notice, mostly through word of mouth. Friends placed the book in stores in Seattle, then throughout California, and as far away as London.

As sales grew, Tolle and Kellough tried to make a distribution arrangement with an established publisher, but twice the deal fell through. Tolle was ready to quit, Kellough writes, but she encouraged him to try one more time. This time they were able to come to an agreement with the owner of a Bay Area publishing company, New World Library, who sensed something special about *The Power of Now* and agreed to buy the rights to it. The first U.S. printing of seventy-five hundred copies sold out in three months.[32]

Even that relatively small act of going public brought Tolle to the attention of the ideaplex, which, as we know, is ever on the prowl for new ideas and idea creators, and in particular one of its major figures, Oprah Winfrey. The book struck her powerfully. She gave it a mention in the November 2000 issue of *O, the Oprah Magazine*, causing a sales spike of some sixty-five thousand copies.[33]

The Power of Now proved to be something more than just another book recommendation for Oprah. She chose to feature it on her preholiday special, "Favorite Things." Orders went through the roof,[34] and some three hundred thousand copies of the book were sold in a short period of time.[35] *The Power of Now* hit number one on the Amazon list and spent months as a *New York Times* best-seller. As Tolle's publisher put it, "We consider this the type of book that comes out once in a decade at best, and, probably—given the way the book has performed—once in a lifetime."[36]

Just as a book had transformed Guiliano's life and endeavors, *The Power of Now* transformed Tolle into an idea entrepreneur and eventually brought him enormous worldwide influence. Without it, he might have continued to gain friends and advocates and supporters within his spiritual community, but it took the expression, the sacred expression, to enable him to go public and break out big-time.

BOOK? REALLY?

Many people find it perplexing, and even unbelievable, that the book is still such a favored form of sacred expression. Surely it is possible to go public and break out through social media and live events? It is—as the stories of Hannah Salwen and Cesar Millan demonstrate—but sooner or later, the idea entrepreneur wants a book. Many people have come to me saying, to the effect, "John, people love my blog, I have been tweeting nonstop, I have speaking engagements booked through spring, I just did my talk at the eduinfotainment fest and I got a standing ovation, but I need a book. *I've got to have a book.*"

Here's why.

First and foremost, a nonfiction book is the most natural home and comfortable haven for the complete expression of an idea. Unlike a video, a blog, an article, or a long talk, a book can contain a nuanced and extended argument, relate a complex and detailed narrative, and house a huge amount of accumulated material, including practices, as no other form of expression can. A blog series, for example, does not demand a throughline of thought the way a book does and a talk can stand without a framework.

Even if almost nobody actually reads the nuanced, complex, and detailed expression of the idea, or plows through the entire accumulation, the creation of a book most reliably forces the idea entrepreneur to do the thinking necessary to articulate the idea, develop the framework, and refine the practices—and this work will prove incredibly useful for the creation of all other expressions. Not only can the book provide the backbone for an article, all that material contained therein (whether puffed up or not) can provide the content seeds for countless other blog posts, videos, talks, events, and emblems.

Plus, even those who *don't* read the book in its entirety will know—with even the most casual flipping and dipping—that the detailed, nuanced argument and full narrative does exist there, which counts for a good deal. In this way, the book is proof of what I call "evidence of effort." It is not enough just to make an effort; it is necessary to have proof of the effort that has been made, and a book is surely that. While almost anyone can write a blog or miniblog, not everyone can or does write a book. Even mediocre books take considerable effort to produce. A really good book demonstrates that the author is serious, is willing to step forward and claim an idea, has a degree of confidence in it, and has accumulated enough material to fill many pages. "When you write a book," Martha Stewart said about the publication of her first book, *Entertaining*, "you're an expert and people look at you in a different way."[37]

The book takes on even greater value if there is some agony and suffering and great trial—or at the very least some struggle and challenge—involved in creating it such that the writing of the book becomes part of the personal narrative. I have collaborated with at least three authors over the years, people of generally good health, who developed severe physical ailments during the book-writing process. One of them endured intense back troubles and could only write lying down. Another suffered a perforated intestine and underwent emergency surgery. A third, who had been working on his book for almost a decade, fell into a coma and was pronounced dead three times. He miraculously recovered and, as soon as he was able, went right back to work on the book. It was published two years later.

The book also has value as a legal document, a title of ownership to the ideas contained therein, a contract between writer, publisher, reader, and the world at large. As faulty and contested as the copyright laws may be in this country (especially with the controversy around books being scanned into digital databases), and as oft-violated as they are, they still have teeth—and far sharper ones than those of other countries, such as China, India, and Russia. Copyright is especially important today when anything posted anywhere on the web is considered fair game by just about anyone for copying, adapting, forwarding, and linking to, if not outright stealing.

First-time authors still get goose bumps when they open their brand-new book to the copyright page and see the line "Copyright © by Me," which is often followed by the Library of Congress Cataloging-in-Publication Data and the official International Standard Book Number (ISBN).

Finally, the physical book is perhaps the most perfect concretization of an abstraction. The idea is the book, the book is the idea. And to make it even more appealing, the book remains one of the most successful technologies and appealing objects ever created. People adore books. They are easy to use and incredibly versatile. People love the way books look, feel, and smell. What other form of expression is such a wonderful combination of object and content? A book's glory as an object is likely to become even more important, as more and more text is delivered online and through electronic readers, and the physical object becomes more rare.

TALKING

Writing is an essential form of expression for the idea—in book, blog, tweet, article, or other—but it is the rare idea entrepreneur (I can't think of one) who does not also employ other forms of expression to hand on her ideas and infect the minds of others, and the most important of those is, of course, talking.

That's because for all its virtues, the book—indeed, any form of writing—also has some significant limitations. It is one-way and fixed. It places the entire burden of apprehension on the reader. Its delivery method is limited to words on a page or screen. (Let's leave out the various forms of "enhanced" electronic books for the moment.) The book cannot respond to the immediate circumstances in which it is being consumed. Books cannot communicate through animal magnetism or pheromonal attraction. So, there are reasons that some people think of books as dry and dusty and out of touch with the real world. *Book larnin'*.

Today, more than ever, the idea entrepreneur must be bi-expressionary. You must write, in forms short and long, and you must talk. On big stages and in break-out rooms. In videos and radio interviews. In panel discussions and special events. And the talking must not be just an oral version of the written words, a recitation of what was in the book or article, because that is not the point of talking.

I remember attending a talk by Malcolm Gladwell not long after *The Tipping Point* was published. I had recently read the book and was surprised when Gladwell began his talk with the same story that opened the book and proceeded to deliver what was essentially a severely condensed version of what he had already written. For those who had not read the book, the talk may have been fine. I found it a disappointment. I wanted to hear *about* the book, get more on his personal narrative, hear how Gladwell related the ideas in the book to things that were going on at that moment. Only in the question-and-answer period, which continued during an informal session in the bar, did the audience get additional material that added to their understanding of the content of the book.

Gladwell is hardly alone in this practice (and he may well have changed it). Many authors think of their presentation as a "book talk," meaning that it is just another way of delivering the words on the page. This is usually a less-than-satisfactory experience for all involved. The author feels frustrated that he must leave so much out; the audience feels annoyed that the author is trying to cram so much in.

The most obvious feature of talking that writing does not provide is the physical presence of the idea entrepreneur. The amount of information, both intellectual and emotional, that is contained within a person's physical appearance, facial expressions, hand gestures and bodily movements, vocal tone, accent, fluency of delivery, and ability to respond to situations and circumstances is immense. But the process of seeing and processing all this visual and aural information consumes a considerable percentage of the listener's energy, so there is less energy available for the real-time processing of the idea, which means that the speaker needs to employ all the oratorical skills—including repetition and vocal emphasis—to ensure that the feelings and emotions are handed on to the listener.

So the two forms—writing and speaking—are complementary and additive, and the combination of the two delivers the fullest understanding of the idea and the most vivid presentation of the fascination and personal narrative.

Exquisite Intonations

Every idea entrepreneur achieves his or her own distinctive balance of writing and speaking, which has an immediate effect on how each is perceived and also has a long-range effect on their influence.

For a little perspective on this issue, let me return for a moment to Ralph Waldo Emerson, worker of the nineteenth-century ideaplex. Emerson was a star on the circuit and people swooned when they heard him. Of one speech that Emerson gave, a woman wrote a published account, saying, "[I]f you have never heard Mr. Emerson when speaking in public, you can have no idea of the effect which his personal appearance and delivery give to his thought. Imagine a face, expressive, alike, of great intellectual power and sweetness of nature; eyes, which, at times, seem to look into another world with far-seeing and prophetic ken; a mouth of chiseled beauty, which never speaks but to utter the most melodious—the most exquisite intonations of which the English language is capable."[38]

At least for this audience member, Emerson had an ability to perform such that he could, in Tolstoyan fashion, hand on his emotions in a way that others felt them, then and there. As James Elliot Cabot writes in *A Memoir of Ralph Waldo Emerson* regarding a speech Emerson gave in Boston, the audience came "to hear Emerson, not to hear his opinions."[39] He continues of the audience that they "liked to put themselves under the influence of one who obviously had lived the heavenly life from his youth up, and who made them feel for the time as if that were the normal mode of existence."[40]

In their talking, idea entrepreneurs have an ability to animate their idea and communicate their personal narrative through their presence and delivery. They are also canny structuralists, and Emerson again established a model: this one for how to construct a powerful speech. He would center his lecture around a fundamental issue or problem of the day—such as society, manners, or ethics—that was general enough to be adapted or pushed in a variety of different directions, depending on the occasion.

The talk would be composed of a series of prepared short segments, made possible by his considerable accumulation of material—anecdotes, thoughts, bits of analysis, references, biographies, focusing facts, stories—that could be updated as events occurred and the environment shifted, selected or customized slightly to suit a particular audience, and made shorter or longer to suit the event.[41] This approach served him well throughout his speaking career. Add PowerPoint, some interactive graphics, and a few video clips and you will find that most successful public speakers, and the best idea entrepreneurs, still address their audiences in essentially the same way.

The downside of Emerson's focus on the lecture as his sacred expression is that he tended to think in the reverse of the "book talk." That is, he seemed to view his prose writings as talks captured in their second-best form. The result is that, as John Updike writes, "The very agility with which Emerson's pithy, exhortative sentences dance to keep the listener's attention wearies the reader now."[42] What sings from the lectern, in other words, may feel like a drag on the page.

Emerson actually had mixed feelings about both forms of expression. According to his biographer, James Elliot Cabot, Emerson believed that his most sacred expression was neither the lecture nor the essay. It was poetry.[43]

Public Appearances

Talking can become the dominant activity for the idea entrepreneur, usually done, at least at first, in interviews and appearances related to the sacred expression (such as a book tour) as well as at established conferences, retreats, seminars, and the like that are managed by an organization of some kind (the eduinfotainment venues I have discussed such as TED, Aspen, SXSW, 92nd Street Y, Nobels Colloquia, and on and on).

Indeed, because speaking can be so lucrative and so useful in building audiences and gathering friends and creating respiration, many idea entrepreneurs think of their writing, especially the book, as primarily a way to get onto the speaking circuit or to amp up the level of their activity there.

After some time, however, the conventional lecture circuit tends to lose its appeal. You may come to feel like the hired help, the celebrity wheeled in to deliver a keynote after-dinner speech, lead a panel discussion, and be available for grip-and-grin photos. You may have little control over the circumstances and too often find yourself coming into a room "cold" and trying to connect with an audience that is completely unfamiliar to you.

So, when the stresses start to outweigh the benefits, and when the sacred expression has been successful enough that you can attract an audience entirely on your own, the nature of the talking can shift to special events. No more being carted in as the outside attraction among the executive speakers; no more sharing the stage with ten or a hundred other idea promoters at the annual idea fest.

Eckhart Tolle has developed one of the most complex and fascinating live presences of any idea entrepreneur. He offers several types of engagements that are carefully categorized as "talks," "intensives," and "retreats."[44] At some of these, Tolle appears live; others are led by his personal and professional partner (a.k.a. wife), Kim Eng. Many of them are recorded.

The live talks typically feature Tolle on stage, sometimes with a moderator. He does not have an electric presence like Cesar Millan or Ralph Waldo Emerson, but it is powerful nonetheless. (I have not attended a live event, but have watched them on video.) Tolle speaks softly, his voice intimate and his manner casual. You do not feel that he is delivering a lecture. He often pauses to think through what he wants to say. Sometimes he stumbles on a word, but he speaks lucidly and with sincerity, as well as with kindness and politeness. There is time for questions and for dialogue. Tolle truly engages with his audience members, and the result can be electric. It is not as if Tolle is delivering a fixed answer to a rote question, but rather trying to find a solution to a problem. In these engagements, Tolle is in the moment, as if he is learning as much as the audience is.

Tolle's intensives and retreats, by contrast, do not take place in a hall or studio. They feature Tolle in a campus or resort setting and typically involve another teacher and a variety of practices and activities. The agenda features lots of time in silence, free moments to do as you please, and daily sessions with Meister Eckhart.

In addition to these events, Tolle also makes special appearances, some of which are with people who have influence in other fields and can expose him to different audiences. In 2009, for example, Tolle spoke at the Vancouver Peace Summit with five Nobel laureates, including the Dalai Lama.[45] Tolle was also a host and speaker at the Global Alliance for Transformational Entertainment (GATE) conference in Los Angeles, a gathering of power players in the entertainment industry, along with actor Jim Carrey.[46]

In all of the recordings I have seen, Tolle in no way resembles the kind of overexposed speaker one might engage through a speakers' bureau. Even Bill Clinton, whom I heard speak at a private corporate gathering, could not escape giving the impression—as fantastic a speaker as he is—that he was not fully in the moment, that this engagement was just one of many he had given that week (possibly that day), and that it was unlikely he was expecting to learn anything from the audience.

An Unlikely Expression

Although a TED appearance may have become the gold standard of the public talk, it owes its rise—at least in part—to the amazing success of a presentation that began with, of all things, a Power-

Point lecture. I speak, of course, of the presentation given by Al Gore, who is the former vice president of the United States, a Nobel Prize laureate, the lead figure in an Academy Award–winning documentary, and author of the best-selling book version of this idea, which goes by the same title.

Gore's idea is fundamentally in line with Thoreau's—that we have to live more simply and in better harmony with nature—with the present-day update that, if we don't, we're going to destroy our planet. (Thoreau made the same admonition, but, even in his warnings about the intrusion of railroads and the rapacious habits of commercial ice cutters, he didn't predict complete planetary doom.)

Gore, of course, had been fascinated with this topic for years, even in his days as an undergraduate at Harvard, and so can claim a long and rich period of accumulation. In 1992, Gore published *Earth in the Balance: Forging a New Common Purpose*, developed after he lost his first presidential bid, in 1988. The PowerPoint presentation, which he began delivering after his election defeat in 2000, built on the success of that book and created more exposure for his ideas. The application of Gore's talking presence to the messages of the book made the ideas more appealingly human—especially considering that his personal narrative was the stuff of worldwide headline news—but I would not say that Gore matched the exquisite intonations of Emerson nor did he offer the mouth of chiseled beauty. Still, he had the will and the conviction, and the lecture was effective.

Gore expanded his talking into video in a way that few idea entrepreneurs have done. He produced, with filmmaker Davis Guggenheim, the documentary feature called *An Inconvenient Truth*. The film won two Oscars at the 2006 Academy Awards—one for Best Documentary Feature and the second for Best Original Song.

Gore followed up the lecture and movie with the book, *An Inconvenient Truth: The Planetary Emergency of Global Warming and*

What We Can Do About It (Rodale, 2006), which sold hundreds of thousands of copies and spawned two more books. In 2007, Gore won the Nobel Peace Prize for his efforts. That almost puts him in company with playwright George Bernard Shaw (1856–1950), who is the only person to have won both an Oscar and a Nobel Prize. Gore didn't technically win the Oscar since Guggenheim was the director of the documentary.[47]

Even for all the success of the documentary and his books, Gore's sacred expression remains that PowerPoint talk. The movie added more of Gore's personal narrative (although it was more traditionally biographical than a depiction of iconic moments and revelations) and so was able to transfer emotions in a way that is beyond the range of a slide show. The companion book, however, seemed more like a printed version of the presentation, just as Emerson's books echoed his lectures. Indeed, Michiko Kakutani, in her *New York Times* review of *An Inconvenient Truth*, wrote that "its roots as a slide show are very much in evidence."[48]

EMBLEMS

To writing and talking, we can add one other, slightly less essential expression: emblems. An emblem, according to the Oxford English Dictionary, is "[a] picture of an object (or the object itself) serving as a symbolical representation of an abstract quality, an action, state of things, class of persons, etc."[49]

House in the Woods

An emblem may seem tangential to an idea or too superficial to have the ability to transfer feelings to others, but the right emblem can bring a lot to the idea and can also serve as a potent mnemonic.

Over time, especially, emblems can build up tremendous resonance. Such is the case with the image of Thoreau's self-built house at Walden Pond, which appears on the cover of the original edition of *Walden*. It is a signature emblem and it expresses the essence of Thoreau's idea: the individual, alone, in nature, living deliberately. It's hard not to be drawn in by it.

Particularly because Thoreau himself is not pictured, the emblem of the house seems ready to open its doors to us and our thoughts. *I, too, have always wished to live deliberately. I, too, could imagine myself living apart in the woods. I, too, am a creature of nature who feels disaffected from, yet unable to completely separate myself from, the comforts and delights of civilization.* The cabin image does not mean more than the book, nor does it dumb down the idea. It leads the reader into the narrative, takes on more and more meaning through the reading of the book, and stays in the mind long after engagement with any of Thoreau's expressions. It is even more meaningful when you learn that the black-and-white image was created by Thoreau's sister, Sophia, rather than by a commercial artist commissioned by the publisher. It is the genuine article. Plus, as no doubt pleased Thoreau, it cost nothing to create.

Boundary Objects

Like the image of Thoreau's house, the powerful emblem is not only expressive and memorable, it is also flexible and adaptable and can accommodate many interpretations. It is porous or, in the parlance of experts in social change, an emblem such as Thoreau's house might be called a "boundary object"— that is, a tangible that appeals and beckons to people across disciplines and ideologies, and brings them together.

In that house, many different kinds of people—including writers, naturalists, survivalists, social justice liberals, builders, teachers, environmentalists, scientists, and antitax conservatives—find meaning. The house celebrates American individualism. It suggests self-sufficiency. It is a writer's garret, a naturalist's outpost, the iconoclast's declaration of separation. It is a blow to the conformity of the typical life path of family and work. It's a shrine to the importance of community. Almost whatever you wish it to be, it is.

Clarity of expression is important for the idea entrepreneur, but porousness—the ability for an expression to embrace many meanings and messages—is also valuable.

Deliberate or Found

Emblems can be deliberately created, but they are more often found or generated during the course of accumulation, and become emblematic through use and constant application. Not every idea entrepreneur has an emblem, or at least not one that really strikes a chord, but those who do are blessed, because an emblem has a remarkable ability to encapsulate, represent, and embody an idea and an idea entrepreneur in an efficient way.

This is the case with the pyramid image usually associated with Maslow's hierarchy of needs framework. Maslow himself did not create or use the pyramid emblem; it developed into the signature emblem for his central idea that human needs are arranged in a kind of escalating stack, with the most difficult to achieve at the pinnacle.

Another example of an emblem that is at the very center of the idea is the black swan, which is also the title of Nassim Nicholas Taleb's book, *The Black Swan*. His idea is that anomalies and highly improbable phenomena, such as black swans, have a far greater impact on us than we think and we should spend more time learning about them, preparing for them, and taking advantage of them.

Idea entrepreneurs often deliberately attempt to create an emblem for their idea, but it's difficult to do. An emblem is not a logo or a symbol. It has to connect with the idea in a way that is instantly understandable and deeply resonant on a number of levels.

Mireille Guiliano attributes some of the appeal of her books to the cover image, which serves as an emblem for the French sense of *joie de vivre*. It depicts a perky, slim young woman prancing along a street, the leash of her perky slim dog in one hand, a roller bag containing the essential elements of the French lifestyle—champagne, baguette, and flowers—in the other. It is an image that Guiliano commissioned (having rejected the publisher's design), and it has become her signature emblem.

The Napoleon Drawing

Perhaps the most striking emblem associated with the idea entrepreneurs in this book is the "Napoleon drawing" that has become closely associated with Edward Tufte. It appeared in Tufte's first book, *The Visual Display of Quantitative Information*; he still discusses it in his one-day course; and it has become a durable manifestation of his ideas—so identified with Tufte (despite the fact that he didn't create it) that even people who haven't read a word of his books often identify him as the "guy with that Napoleon chart."

The drawing depicts the march of Napoleon's army into Moscow in the winter of 1812. It was created by Charles Joseph Minard (1781–1870), who was not an artist, but a civil engineer. From the image on that 20" x 22" sheet, in just two colors, tan and black, you quickly comprehend the horrifying story. A thick, optimistic line of French soldiers marches toward Moscow; a rapidly narrowing line of defeated, dispirited, dying soldiers retreats. It's a map, spreadsheet, narrative, and work of art all in one. Tufte writes, "It may well be the best statistical graphic ever drawn."[50]

Many of Tufte's ideas and practices are evident in the Minard drawing, and now he and it are inextricably connected.

TIMING

Every idea is contained differently in the mixture and sequence of expressions, and every idea entrepreneur gains influence differently as a result of how the expressions are received.

The power-of-half endeavor, for example, for all its success, had an interesting feature: the book, even with all that attention, did not perform up to expectations. The Africa project went well. The Salwens did their fair share of talking. But, as of this writing, two years after publication, *The Power of Half* has sold about fifteen thousand copies in the United States. This is perfectly respectable—many authors would be pleased with such sales—but the sales performance has not matched the reception the book received from the ideaplex. And it's doubtful that the profits enabled the publisher to recoup its substantial advance.

There are several possible reasons for this. One is that the Salwen's sacred expression is actually the philanthropic practice: they made a firm commitment to selling their house and donating the proceeds to charity and they lived up to that pledge and then some. The book, therefore, was a secondary expression.

Another reason for the book's less-than-stellar performance may be its timing. The Salwens placed the book with a publisher before they had sold the house, before they knew what the effect of their charitable contributions would be, and before they really could evaluate the effect of the project on family dynamics. Indeed, Hannah told us that the project had taken a toll on her personal life, especially her relationships with her classmates, some of whom questioned her motives and thought the whole project was actually a scheme to make her famous and get her into a good college.

Timing was also an issue in regard to the accumulation of material. Hannah, after all, was only fourteen. The project itself was less than two years old when the Salwens stepped into the public arena. They simply had not had enough time to gather lots of material, synthesize it, analyze it, create a framework, and develop a set of practices that others could follow. Yes, they made suggestions—such as volunteering half the hours that you spend online and the like—but the main practice, shedding your most precious possession, is a hard one to replicate.[51]

The personal narrative is also a bit perplexing, and that may be because of timing as well. The book is cowritten by Hannah and Kevin and, apart from the iconic moment at the stoplight, their narratives seem quite different. Kevin's fascination, he says, is about family dynamics. Hannah's is more about social inequality. Kevin is looking inward, while Hannah is more focused on her environment. Although the differing perspectives add richness, it can also feel that their motivations for going public are at odds. *Why now?*

All these factors—the forms of expression, the way the expressions emerge, and the timing of going public—have an important effect on another essential aspect of idea entrepreneurship: respiration.

4

RESPIRATION

As you explore your fascination, accumulate material, create expressions, and build a personal narrative, something may begin to happen around you and your idea: *respiration*.

This, as we'll see, can be exciting, sometimes unexpected, and even nerve-wracking.

By respiration, I mean that the idea starts to breathe and take on a life of its own. A simple way to think about respiration: it's when other people start creating their own expressions about your expressions. They talk about the idea. They write about it. They incorporate it or make reference to it in their own books, speeches, blogs, articles, and videos.

Respiration is the sum total of expressions about the idea.

It is through respiration that ideas disseminate, yes, but more than that, it is how they are refined, detailed, strengthened, and applied. Respiration is the process by which people take an idea on board, consider it, and make it their own. It is the route to influence.

The idea entrepreneur cannot *force* respiration. You cannot command people to talk about your idea, require them to adopt your practices, demand that they make reference to what you have to say. You cannot make people think how you want them to think or behave as you want them to behave.

Still, it is possible to create conditions that are conducive to respiration, to jump-start it, and to keep it going.

The most obvious and sure way to generate respiration is to create a hit expression. A much-read blog. A viral video. A popular talk. A well-reviewed or best-selling book. A single hit expression can create a lot of respiration, and that may be all that's necessary to have your idea break out, and for you to build influence.

Unfortunately, it is almost impossible to intentionally create a hit of any kind. So your goal should simply be to create the sacred expression—the strongest, most complete, authoritative, all-in version that combines all the elements we have discussed, including personal narrative, framework, and practices. If it becomes a hit, even within a single audience group, that's all to the good. If it does not, it can still be an important step in the furthering of your idea.

The creation of a solid expression may sound like an obvious goal, but I have come across any number of would-be idea entrepreneurs who seem to think that it is sufficient only to *have* an expression—any expression—and to just "get it out there," as if it is only the existence of an expression that matters, not the quality of it, not what goes into it. *I just need a book. I just have to have a speech. I could really use a logo.*

The odds are that expressions created in this way will be neither hits nor useful to the idea entrepreneur in gaining influence for the idea. Any audience will catch the whiff of the hasty, cynical, incomplete, or ingenuine expression and will turn up their noses. They will not breathe in. Respiration will not occur.

RISKING IT

You can go public with an expression but do so in a way that limits your exposure to people and their sometimes irksome questions and responses; to create respiration you must become part of the conversation. You have to put yourself into the fray—listen, engage, respond, take your lumps. There is risk involved. Weaknesses in your idea may be exposed. Assumptions may be questioned. Your personal narrative will come under scrutiny. You may even, although it's not likely, face physical peril.

Kiran Bedi knows all of this very well. Although many Western readers have likely not heard of her, Bedi has become one of India's leading voices for an approach to the management of prisons, prisoners, and rehabilitation, which she calls *collaborative correction*. Punishment accomplishes nothing for anybody, she says, and a penal system (in India or anywhere; she has considerable influence worldwide) should rehabilitate criminal offenders rather than punish them.

Underlying her idea about this proper form of correction lies an even more fundamental concern: that India must remove its deep and enduring personal habits of corruption, especially those of government and public officials, and particularly those that are pervasive in the justice system.

Bedi, who was transferred from her post as a prison administrator in 1995, went on to become an idea entrepreneur. She has expressed herself in writing, publishing several books including *I Dare!* (Hay House, 1995) and *It's Always Possible* (Sterling, 1998). She has written articles for the *Hindustan Times* and other Indian dailies. She has lectured at Harvard, Columbia, Oxford, Cambridge, and NYU, and delivered a TED talk that has been viewed tens of thousands of times online.[1] In 2002, Bedi was voted one of India's "most admired" women by *The Week*; in 2005 she was nominated for the Nobel Peace Prize.[2] And in 2010, *Reader's Digest* called her the most trusted woman in India.[3]

Much of this attention stems from Bedi's ability to create respiration around herself and her idea—as she did in the most direct and fundamental way from the very beginning of her most difficult assignment.

In Their Face

In the summer of 2011, Anna and I and our Indian colleague, journalist Mridu Khullar Relph, met with Bedi in her basement office in Delhi. Mridu was especially excited to meet Bedi who has long been a hero of hers. When we arrived, Bedi was finishing up an interview with a television crew with the kind of confidence and casualness of a person well-acquainted with life in the ideaplex and, as the crew packed up, she turned immediately to us and began to tell her story.

In 1972, Kiran Bedi became the first female officer to join the Indian Police Service. Although she had some bumps along the way—as Delhi Police traffic chief in 1982, she towed Prime Minister Indira Gandhi's improperly parked car—she rose in the ranks and, in 1993, was named inspector general (IG) of Tihar Jail, one of the largest prisons in India (and the world), with over nine thousand inmates at the time. Not that the position was any great prize; it had been vacant for months before Bedi was named and no one else was vying for the post. As she writes in her book *It's Always Possible,* she knew the jail was a tough place, characterized by "the gang wars, prisoners running extortion centres from within the prison, and tales of rampant corruption, violence and heart-rending tragedies. But I was a soldier, duty-bound to take charge of this hell-hole."[4]

And so she did. She recounts her first days at Tihar Jail as if they were yesterday—just as you would expect of such an iconic and revelatory time for her. Bedi arrived at her private office on a Saturday to meet with her staff for the first time. She found the office was almost as disgusting as the inmates' cells were reputed to be: dirty, overrun with rodents, buzzing with insects. As she talked, her staff members looked at their new chief with suspicion, shrugged at her overtures and ideas.

So far, so not good.

Next came her introduction to the prison itself. On Monday, May 3, 1993, she determined that her first agenda item would be to meet the inmates. This was not absolutely necessary, but she wanted to directly engage with them, to immediately put a face on her idea and to model it herself. She knew very well that such meetings did not always go well. Some years before, a prisoner had attacked the IG who was making just such a visit and had bitten off the inspector's finger.

Bedi was ushered through the two sets of gates that led into the prison. Each was opened and then closed behind her before the next one was unlocked. She observed that there was not much in the way of security that might help her if things got out of hand— no surveillance cameras, no alarms or emergency communications systems.

Bedi entered the largest ward, where some six hundred inmates were housed. Her audience had gathered in the courtyard. When she appeared, the men beheld a woman of no imposing size (5" 3", 120 pounds) who was dressed, not in boots and official uniform as they might have expected, but in flat shoes and a casual *pathan* suit—loose-fitting trousers and a waist-length Nehru-style jacket.

As Bedi approached them, the inmates moved toward her. They seemed more curious than menacing, but the prison staff was on alert. They brandished their sticks, and motioned for the inmates to sit. They obeyed. Bedi looked over her new charges. "I stood facing them, not knowing what expression would be most suitable for the moment," Bedi writes in her book. What could she expect from them? What would they respond to? What did she wish to convey?

As she told us in our interview, an unusual, untried, and unplanned approach popped into her mind in a flash. She looked at the men, at their blank stares, and found herself blurting out a question.

"Do you pray?"

No answers. What kind of question was that? What was its relevance? The prisoners seemed surprised and confused that their new IG was speaking so directly and personally to them. No speech? No assertion of authority?

She asked the question again. "Do you pray?" Still no answer. She moved closer. She looked them over, then focused on one man. She repeated her question to him.

"Do you pray?"

Under her direct gaze, it seemed impossible for him not to respond. "Yes, sometimes."

This is respiration at its most elemental. Even if she had not expressed her idea in words yet, she had expressed it in her bearing and her action.

"Very good," she said, relieved that she had gotten some small response. She looked back to the group. "Who else does?" Others murmured that, yes, they prayed.

Then Bedi proposed they all pray together. But which prayer? What would everyone know? She thought of a popular song, from a Bollywood movie, that amounts to a prayer and that everybody surely would be familiar with.

"Get up to sing together," Kiran urged the inmates.

Singing? Unusual and unexpected. Some of the prisoners started to stand, but the guards threatened them again.

Bedi overrode them. "I told you to stand up to sing!"

The guards "got the message." Soon the entire ward was standing and singing along, which was about being virtuous and avoiding wrongdoing.[5]

A Multilayered Moment

In that supercharged episode, Bedi had accomplished a lot. She had engaged in a kind of conversation, even though few words were exchanged. She had modeled her practice of collaborative correction. She created an iconic moment that all could remember and relate to others. There could be no doubt that this would be talked about by the inmates, whatever their view of her and the moment might be. Indeed, respiration had begun.

Engagement with the audience that is most immediately and directly affected by your idea is important because, through those people, you speak indirectly to other audiences. In her encounter, Bedi, for example, was essentially talking to other prisoners in other institutions, other members of her own prison staff who were not in the yard that day, as well as prison staff of other institutions in India and around the world.

She had other audiences in mind, too, such as penal institution administrators, government officials, families of prisoners, potential employers of prisoners, and others. These people heard about Bedi's prison encounter, the song, the response from the prisoners, and watched as her idea took effect.

During her two-year tenure at Tihar, the jail became a model for prison reform around the world. The majority of the inmates went home and did not come back. In 1994 Bedi was awarded the Roman Magsaysay Award, which is sometimes referred to as

Asia's Nobel Prize, for her contributions to crime prevention, prison and police reform, and drug rehabilitation.[6]

Bedi's willingness to talk with us, although she did not know us and could easily have ignored our request for an interview, shows that she understands that respiration must continue long after your idea has been introduced. The engagement should never end.

A MUTUALLY ANIMATING PLATFORM

An expression can create respiration on its own but it usually has a greater chance of doing so if it is part of a platform, one of a set of expressions that are *mutually animating*.

A platform of mutually animating expressions is not at all the same as an "integrated marketing campaign" or a coordinated communications effort or media blitz or any similarly conceived and executed initiative that is essentially devised to further and promote a single expression—the book or an event—and in which all the other expressions point back to the central one or simply restate its material.

Mutual animation means that each expression adds more meaning and new detail and additional depth to another expression, while remaining distinct and valuable unto itself. Cesar Millan's books add dimension—largely about his personal narrative, and a framework of his practices—to his television show. You cannot get from Edward Tufte's books what you get from his one-day course or from a discussion thread on his website. Eckhart Tolle delivers in person what cannot unfold on the page. Dining with Mireille Guiliano is a different experience from watching interviews with her on TV.

To illustrate how the expressions can build into a platform, and animate and build on each other, let us briefly return to Ralph

Waldo Emerson, who got the hang of mutual animation as swiftly as he saw the possibilities of the lecture circuit.

A platform was simpler in the nineteenth century than it is now, but the process of building one was essentially the same. First, there comes news in the content venues (i.e., newspapers) that Emerson is to present a lecture at such and such a place. The telegraph may be involved in spreading the word. The announcement generates some respiration among readers of the newspaper and those they connect with. *Ah, Mr. Emerson is coming to town. Have you read his works? I hear he is quite a fellow. Perhaps we should attend? Great intellectual power, mouth of chiseled beauty, and all that.*

Emerson arrives in town. He often stays in the home of a local somebody. They and some number of guests engage in conversation over a meal or a stroll. Word of what was discussed gets out. There is new material contained therein, beyond what is known from his writings and previous lectures. *I hear that Emerson has adjusted his views on English manners somewhat . . .*

The lecture duly occurs. The fifty or hundred or three hundred people who attend carry on a mental conversation with Emerson as he speaks. They bring home his comments and their account of how his feelings were, or were not, expressed and how they responded to them. Those who are listening form their own ideas of Emerson's ideas. *I'm told that Mr. Emerson likens the individual Englishman to an island, just as England itself is an island. Interesting . . .*

Members of the local commentariat, who have also attended, report on the lecture in their content venues. Their ideas about Emerson's ideas are further cause for respiration. *Did you hear what the* Herald of Freedom *had to say about . . . ?* Some newspapers decide that interest in Emerson is great enough (or the amount of available space is large enough) that it makes sense to reprint his speech in its entirety. Although this has its benefits for Emerson and his ideas, because it reaches a wider audience than the speech itself could, reprinting also concerns Emerson for the very reason that it is not so good for the cause of mutual animation. The publication of the full speech in the newspaper might reduce interest in the next book, which would be based on the speech. *I've already read it.*

That is how it went for Emerson. Once he saw the pattern, he began to organize his speaking engagements so they would become, in addition to moments of expression, opportunities for accumulation. In 1847, for example, Emerson was invited by the Mechanics' Institutes in Lancashire and Yorkshire, England, to deliver a series of lectures there. He would be paid enough to cover the expenses of an extensive trip through England and Scotland and there would also be, as he put it, a "home and a committee of intelligent friends awaiting me in every town."[7] This put Emerson in a position to participate in conversations with well-connected people who might become endorsers and who would also build respiration about him, his life, his lectures, and his ideas.

While in the United Kingdom, as he was chatting with intelligent friends around the dinner table and exhorting at the lectern, Emerson was collecting impressions, ideas, and stories. He eventually built them into a series of essays that he called *English Traits.* This provided him with content for a new series of lecture dates back home in America and, in due course, he collected the lecture-essays into a book, also called *English Traits,* which he published in 1856, nine years after his original journey to the United Kingdom.

Not only did this intriguing piece of writing expand his audience in the United States, it also brought him more attention in England. The English, it turned out, seemed quite chuffed that America's intellectual star was writing about their habits, and *English Traits* was widely reviewed in the British press. Many pieces about Emerson and his work appeared, greatly expanding his audience in Europe.[8]

Just this one mutually animating, self-fueling cycle of activity kept Emerson busy for more than a decade. In total, he continued his idea entrepreneurship, thanks to his mutually animating platform of expressions, for almost forty years, from 1833 to 1872.

The hit expression and the mutually reinforcing platform of expressions can create a good deal of respiration, but it naturally lessens over time—as new ideas come on the scene, other expressions become hits, and events occur.

The world in the way it was at the time the expressions were created is rarely the world into which they are launched so they must continue to create respiration. And, as everything changes incessantly faster, the gap between the expressions, the platform, and the world around them seems to yawn more widely. The zeitgeist—the spirit of the times—changes, events occur, the personal narrative moves on.

So the idea entrepreneur must find ways to maintain a *current presence,* and all of the immediate, web-based expressions—the blog, tweet, Facebook posting, e-mail blast, video link—are the most obvious methods of doing so. These expressions enable the idea entrepreneur to adapt and adjust and expand the idea to the zeitgeist as it changes, moment by moment.

Direct Engagement

The simplest, most direct, and usually most powerful form of current presence is showing up—in person—and engaging with live audiences, in large or small groups—just as Kiran Bedi showed up for her most essential audience, the prison population. Preferably the engagements include some kind of interaction, so you can explain, interpret, and personalize your idea in the light of specific issues and individual circumstances and emerging situations, on the spot.

If respiration occurs in the room, it is likely to continue outside the room, as the people who were there write, talk, and think about you and your idea. The audience will have experienced the idea as you experienced it—and will make an effort to continue the expression of it to others. If nothing happens in the room, the prospects for continued respiration are dim.

One particularly effective way to create respiration through live engagement is to engage with the members of an audience that is most immediately and deeply affected by your idea, just as Bedi did, although putting yourself in danger may not be necessary. For this core audience, the idea is not of casual interest, but rather at the center of their lives or professions and inextricably connected to their thinking and behaviors. If they buy your idea, it is likely that other audiences will take note.

Bryant Terry, for example, started off on his journey to idea entrepreneurship by engaging directly with inner-city kids— cooking together and talking about the connection between nutrition and social justice. Tufte puts himself in a room with information designers for six hours at a stretch. Guiliano sits down to dinner with women struggling with their weight. Cesar Millan goes for walks with dogs and their owners.

AUDIENCE AWARENESS

Another benefit of direct engagement is that it allows you to look the audience members in the eye, not only to better deliver the message, but also to see who they are. It can be surprisingly difficult to have a full understanding of who your audience is, especially when so much of the connection is indirect. Just who are those people who are buying the book, posting comments on the blog, or watching the YouTube video? Through direct engagement—

including live events, conversations, and the exchange of personal e-mail—you can see and hear the people who share your fascination and are captured by your ideas. You often discover that the audience is not what you expected or that you are reaching multiple audiences. This understanding has an effect on the further accumulation of material and, indeed, on the creation of new expressions: *As I learned from a woman who attended my talk last week . . . As a guy said to me in an e-mail . . .*

Mireille Guiliano, for example, knew her immediate audience very well: the women who attended her talks around the country and with whom she shared wine, dinner, and conversation, plus her American friends who were never happy with their relationship with food. So she naturally assumed that the audience for her first book would be almost entirely composed of well-educated, affluent women in their forties, a large percentage of them in full-time jobs, who were in emotional and psychological battle with their eating habits and were also probably Francophiles—the kind of women she had been helping for years. And, indeed, those women did buy her book and respond to her. Guiliano knows because she got e-mails from them, engaged with them at talks, and met them at events.

But as she learned from her direct engagement with audiences at venues around the world—and from correspondence, mostly e-mail—her idea also resonated with many other people who were not in the seminal group but who were struggling with the more fundamental underlying issues.

The other groups included younger women—particularly those in their twenties and thirties. Guiliano also heard from kids, like the seven-year-old girl from Florida who wrote to say that, as a result of what she learned from Guiliano, she had made it her mission to get her friends to lay off the McDonald's meals. And she was also connecting with older women, like the eighty-eight-year-old

Midwestern woman who said that Guiliano's book reminded her of the lessons that her parents, who grew up in Sweden, had taught her.

Perhaps most interesting and unexpected, Guiliano received a large number of communications from mothers with young children. "I didn't have children, so I didn't realize what young women were feeding their kids," Guiliano told us. "But I see it with my little nieces—they don't know the difference between a brownie and a broccoli." These busy young parents were struggling with issues of health, diet, and lifestyle for the whole family.

Then Guiliano realized that her appeal was not limited to American women or even to women in developed countries. After her appearance on *Oprah,* Guiliano was flooded with e-mails from people around the world, including South Africa, Australia, the countries of eastern Europe, and even some in the Middle East.

Guiliano also learned that she was reaching men. Many couples were reading her books, presumably with the woman passing the book along to her male partner, and both were putting her ideas into practice. What's more, Guiliano developed a gay following, which became particularly evident when she made appearances at live events such as book fairs in Florida and California.

When an idea entrepreneur reaches multiple audiences, it is evidence that the idea pertains to an essential human need, addresses an important social issue, and connects to a fascination that many others share. Guiliano is about weight loss and the French lifestyle, of course, but more deeply, she is about self-control and self-management, and eating is one of the most basic manifestations of those characteristics.

Guiliano's direct engagement with these audiences has affected how she thinks about her audience, what kind of material she accumulates, and how she develops new expressions. Her understanding of her audience is one of the reasons she followed up

French Women Don't Get Fat with *French Women for All Seasons* and *Women, Work, and the Art of Savoir Faire: Business Sense and Sensibility*, which adapted her ideas particularly for working women. Then came the *French Women Don't Get Fat Cookbook* and now she is completing a book on aging with attitude. These last two books were inspired by requests from her readers and friends.

Hidden

Then there are audiences that are neither obvious nor even directly interested in the main idea. They are, instead, attracted by some subsidiary, tangential, or even hidden aspect of the idea.

Cesar Millan has an obvious audience: dog owners and dog lovers. But through engagement with his audiences, particularly the people who applied to appear with their dogs on his show, it became clear that his idea is more fundamental than the "presenting" issues of dogs (chewing, biting) and even deeper than the issue of pack behavior. Millan is talking, although indirectly, about the behavior of the human pack, particularly its younger members.

Millan, the dirty dog kid who didn't quite fit in with his peers in Mexico, learned that his fascination with dogs and their pack behaviors was relevant to kids—especially those who did not fit the norm—and their relationships with their friends, non-friends, and schoolmates. His work, Millan told us, has inspired legions of young people. "There's a lot more kids that *don't* feel being part of the pack than kids who are popular." By watching Millan's show, reading his books, and attending his events, the younger members of his audience began to understand themselves differently. "You can actually lead your own world, be the pack leader of your own world," he said, "then you can make right choices."

Gradually, because of his engagement with the audience and the respiration he participated in, Millan began to shift his attention to this previously hidden audience. "Grown-ups respond to the book, but to influence or to inspire, motivate, the next generation, which is what is going to rule the country eventually, is really important."

Perhaps that audience understanding eventually led to the development of *Leader of the Pack,* the show that premiered in 2012 after *The Dog Whisperer* had finished its run.

Secret

In addition to these audiences, there is often another audience that I find particularly intriguing, one I think of as a *secret* audience. This is the audience, sometimes an individual, that you— often without fully realizing it—want urgently to connect with, usually on a personal level. You may not be fully aware of who this is, or may know but not be willing to reveal the identity, and you may not always be sure just why this audience is so important to you. Sometimes the secret audience is not a member of the immediate audience or doesn't fit into the wider audience. Sometimes it is someone close, such as a parent, a lover, a colleague, a mentor or hero. It can be a rival or a denigrator. It may not be an individual; it can be an institution or entity or group.

I always ask my clients who their secret audience is. Some know and are willing tell me—*my father/mother* or *my third-grade teacher* or *that jerk boss who said I'd never amount to anything*—while others don't know or won't tell. But I believe that every idea entrepreneur, and every successful expression, has a secret audience and that it's useful to try to figure out who it is.

I asked Hannah Salwen about her secret audience. Who was the book intended for? "We really were writing for the school that my brother goes to," she told Anna and me. "Those moms and people that realize that they have a lot and realize that they're really lucky, and don't realize that they can make an impact." Salwen was referring to the Westminster Schools in Atlanta, a Christian-focused day school for grades K through 12, which some people describe as a pressure cooker, a place where high achievers and school lovers excel and those who are less into academics may not be so happy.

It's important to identify your secret audience, because whoever it is may not share the concerns of your other audiences. If the secret one is too much in your mind, it can confuse the expression. I worked with an author for several years while he struggled to develop a book based on his popular talk. When he spoke, he seemed angry at something or somebody, as if he considered them unable to grasp his idea, even though his idea was meant to be helpful to a large audience of business managers. I finally asked him who he was talking to and why he seemed so angry at them. He couldn't or wouldn't tell me. The book will be out soon; maybe he'll tell me after publication.

CONVERGENCE

Another way that respiration occurs is through convergence—in time and in content—with the zeitgeist, the spirit of the times. Yes, we have been talking about the importance of connecting to fundamental human issues (wellness, self-control, spirituality, relationships), but I am referring here to stuff that is in the news and at the top of the collective mind—those large, troublesome, controversial, simmering societal issues that dominate the ideaplex.

Such was the case with Amy Chua, the so-called Tiger Mother, author of *Battle Hymn of the Tiger Mother* (Penguin, 2011). In her case, the convergence seemed entirely deliberate, if not entirely of her own intent—and came about as the result of the particular excerpt of her book that was published in the *Wall Street Journal*.

As a result of the excerpt, and then the book and her live engagements, I have rarely seen the kind of respiration—more accurately, the hyperventilation—that developed around Chua's idea, which is, essentially, that a certain kind of traditional Chinese parenting, with an emphasis on discipline and the learning of "hard" skills, produces greater long-term success for children than the liberal, touchy-feely American style.

Although Chua is a known figure in academia—she is the John M. Duff Professor of Law at Yale Law School—and had written two previous books (one of which, *World on Fire: How Exporting Free Market Democracy Breeds Ethnic Hatred and Global Instability,* she describes as a *New York Times* best-seller, and that had U.S. sales in the range of fifty thousand copies), I had not been aware of her.

Until, that is, a Saturday morning in January of 2011. I was perusing the weekend edition of the *Journal* when I came across an article with the unignorable title "Why Chinese Mothers Are Superior" and the reading line, "Can a regimen of no playdates, no TV, no computer games and hours of music practice create happy kids? And what happens when they fight back?"

I read. I gulped. I called out to my wife. "Nancy, you have to read this." I read aloud the first lines. "A lot of people wonder how Chinese parents raise such stereotypically successful kids. They wonder what these parents do to produce so many math whizzes and music prodigies, what it's like inside the family, and whether they could do it too. Well, I can tell them, because I've done it."[9]

The editors of the *Wall Street Journal* had clearly chosen a selection from the book that would stab a needle into the nerve of the zeitgeist. The China situation was on everybody's minds at the time, especially those of parents with children who might soon be heading off for college and facing competition from Chinese applicants, but also businesspeople who found themselves competing with Chinese companies as never before, as well as virtually every American citizen who could not help but think about the stake China holds in the U.S. economy.

Instant hyperventilation. The online version of the *Journal* article received nearly nine thousand comments, the most any article on the site had ever received since its inception in 1995, and a number that has not been surpassed to date.[10] Many expressed outrage.

But it was a conflicted outrage, which became evident when the *Journal* online ran a poll asking readers which they thought was better: the "Demanding Eastern" parenting model or the "Permissive Western" model. Even though, by our estimate, the clear majority of the comments posted about the original article were negative, nearly two-thirds of the respondents to the poll voted in favor of the Demanding Eastern model.[11]

Dual Engagement

When Chua's book came out, immediately after the *Journal* excerpt, it blew briskly through the ideaplex and was reviewed and featured in many major content venues. *Tiger Mother* landed on the *New York Times* list and remained in the top ten for weeks.

Chua duly engaged, showing up on the *Today* show, *The Colbert Report,* and many others and taking part in a streamed discussion on parenting for wsj.com. Her engagement, however, seemed to add confusion, rather than clarity, to the idea. In her conversations, she did not seem to be quite the fire-breathing, all-certain, China dragon that the *Journal* excerpt had presented. No, she spoke instead of one of her iconic moments, which involved weakness, her own loss of control, and a fear that she might have damaged her relationship with one of her two daughters as a result of her practices. She admitted mistakes and confessed that she had, over time, come to accept a more Western view of parenting. She related, in short, a compelling personal narrative that might well have connected with multiple groups of parents. There was also a sense, which she contributed to, that the whole effort was, at least in part, one of satire—she was poking fun at herself and at the whole overly intense parenting conversation.

Serious or satirical, the issue riled up the observers and analysts of the political and cultural scene. Think tanker Charles Murray, the W. H. Brady scholar at the American Enterprise Institute, spoke out in favor of Chua. "Large numbers of talented children everywhere would profit from Chua's approach," he wrote. Too many of them, he said, were "frittering away their gifts—they're nice kids, not brats, but they are also self-indulgent and inclined to make excuses for themselves."[12]

Representing the business audience, Donald Trump weighed in, listing Chua's book as one of his "favorite tomes on China."[13] (Was this a compliment or a pan or a joke? I couldn't tell.)

Members of the commentariat had plenty to say. David Brooks, columnist at the *New York Times* and a best-selling author himself, proclaimed that it was Chua, not the Western-style parent, who was "a wimp," arguing that in fact she had been "coddling her children" by shielding them from the harsh social realities of young adulthood. Says Brooks: "Practicing a piece of music for four hours requires focused attention, but it is nowhere near as cognitively demanding as a sleepover with fourteen-year-old girls."[14]

Even Chua's daughters got involved. One of them wrote a letter to her mother in the *New York Post,* entitled, "Why I Love My Strict Chinese Mom." In it, she credits her mother with instilling her with drive and discipline, and teaching her to live her life with purpose, saying, "If I died tomorrow, I would die feeling I've lived my whole life at 110 percent. And for that, Tiger Mom, thank you."[15]

Writer Evan Osnos wanted to know what second-generation Chinese Americans thought about the Tiger Mom. In his *New*

Yorker piece, "Chinese Daughters and Amy Chua," Osnos recounted his conversations with a number of well-educated and accomplished children of immigrants from China. One said that "Chinese mothers are superior in that they equip their children with the skills needed to succeed in their careers and as members of society. However, a different, and more difficult, task for a Chinese mother is to convey their best intentions and love while doing so."[16]

Surfacing a Tension

Martin Luther King understood this phenomenon of hyperventilation very well. Chua, he might have remarked, had "surfaced a tension." In King's famous letter from a Birmingham jail, dated April 16, 1963, he wrote, "We who engage in nonviolent direct action are not the creators of tension. We merely bring to the surface the hidden tension that is already alive." He describes such a tension as a "boil" that must be opened up and brought into the "air of national opinion" if it is to be lanced and removed.[17]

Well, Chua's idea had certainly poked into a number of American boils, including the parlous state of the educational system, our worthiness as parents in the age of social media, and the country's precarious position in the world economy.

Although Chua engaged with her audiences as an author might, she did not behave as an idea entrepreneur would: she seemed to be in need of explaining herself more than exploring the issue. She did not seem to want to build on her idea, expand it, detail it, and suggest ways to adapt and apply it. On her website, Chua writes, "My book has been controversial. Many people have misunderstood it. If I could push a magic button and choose either happiness or success for my children, I'd choose happiness in a second. But I don't think it's as simple as that; it can be a tough world out there, and true self-esteem has to be earned."

Chua did, however, continue to add to the personal narrative. She explains: "I wrote this book in a moment of crisis, when my younger daughter seemed to turn against everything I stood for and it felt like I was losing her and everything was falling apart. After one terrible fight, I sat down at my computer, and even though I usually have writer's block, this time the words just poured out. I showed every page to my daughters and my husband. It was like family therapy."[18]

So what were we to do with that? What feelings was she attempting to hand on? Which moments were the really iconic ones? What practices were we supposed to follow? What to make of her narrative, her motives? Was she really trying to help others, make a difference, change the world? Or was she engaging in what Tolstoy, in *What Is Art?,* called a "game" in which the artist "lets off his excess of stored-up energy"?[19]

Gradually, the hyperventilation around the book lost its intensity and the conversation became more controlled and less strident and then trailed off to relative quietude. Chua had had success with the book in terms of sales (about 155,000 sold in the United States as of late 2012) and plenty of attention in the ideaplex. The book surfaced a tension and created respiration for a short period of time. Whether it changed minds or behaviors, or whether Chua's narrative will become lodged in our minds, is difficult to say. I think of it as an episode and Chua as a venturer into the ideaplex whose idea converged far more violently with the zeitgeist than she might have expected or bargained for. When I mention Chua's name to people now, people tend not to recognize it. But when I say the title of the book, it's a different story. Indeed at a talk I gave to about a hundred people not long ago, few recognized Chua by name. But when I asked if anybody remembered the book *Battle Hymn of the Tiger Mother,* a sharp gasp erupted from the audience. The boil was still there and still lanceable.

PUSHBACK

Chua's adventure also makes the point that respiration can be negative as well as positive. It may often take the form of pushback, rebuttal, rejection, even ridicule and derision. The idea entrepreneur must accept that even these are forms of respiration—expressions created in response to expressions—and not *ad hominem* attacks that warrant revenge.

Indeed, the milder forms of pushback—satire, fun-poking, lampooning, and imitating—are a good indicator that your idea has connected with the zeitgeist and been embraced by the ideaplex. Appearing as a character on *The Simpsons* or *South Park*, getting skewered in the *Onion*, or being included in a list or gallery in the *Daily Beast* is a sign that your idea is being heard and considered, that it has respiration.

Mireille Guiliano has experienced relatively good-natured satire. There are many imitations and takeoffs of her books, including *French Cats Don't Get Fat* by Henry Beard, *Japanese Women Don't Get Old or Fat: Secrets of My Mother's Tokyo Kitchen* by Naomi Moriyama and William Doyle, and *French Women Don't Sleep Alone: Pleasurable Secrets to Finding Love* by Jamie Cat Callan, both of which are actually rather earnest in their intent, and *Gay Men Don't Get Fat,* by Simon Doonan. Guiliano received an e-mail from a friend saying that she should collect a royalty from authors who traded on her title and idea. Guiliano laughed. She was well aware that a lot of people had written books using the words *French women* or the phrase *don't get fat*. She wrote to her friend, "Don't worry. The more clones we have, the better it is."

Indeed, satire and imitation are delightful forms of respiration that throw the original ideas into high relief: they bring out both the defenders and the questioners.

Nastygrams

All too often, however, the fulminations of the undifferentiated, largely unknowable, and certainly uncontrollable "crowd," whose members express themselves primarily on the web, can be surprising, off-putting, and even disturbing.

For the Salwens, for example, the negative stuff began soon after the airing of the *Today* segment that featured them and their Power of Half project, in the summer of 2008. The Salwens liked the piece, but what they didn't like so much were some of the comments about the segment that had been posted on the *Today* show website, which were an indication of things to come. There were plenty of positive comments, as well as some that were mildly critical. One, for example, said Hannah was behaving with "idealistic immaturity." Another called her an "idiot." But there were also a number of "nastygrams," as Kevin called them, calling Hannah foul names ("spoiled whore" among them) and deriding the whole endeavor.[20]

Joan was horrified. Her first impulse was typical of many idea entrepreneurs—to somehow answer the criticism, fight back, make a rebuttal, have the disparagement removed. This is not possible or sensible. In fact, the pushback and ridicule become part of the personal narrative even as it helps shape the idea.

Besides, Hannah and brother Joe were mostly amused, and Kevin took an analytical approach. He suggested they count and categorize the posts, and they found that the positive ones outnumbered the negatives two to one. Not such a bad ratio.

And, just as the *Today* piece had brought out the nastygrams, so did Nicholas Kristof's highly positive blog post about *The Power of Half* in the *New York Times* attract naysayers. Although many commenters praised the Salwens, others questioned why the family wanted to help Africans, rather than Americans, and some did not buy another argument made in the book—that the real benefit of the project was to bring the family closer together.

One commenter, Shana, wrote on Kristof's blog, "Mr. Kristof, I don't know about this. I don't want to pour cold water on generous acts like this, but it sounded as though you were trying to put a spin on this article by exaggerating the benefits the Salwen family received from selling their home. Frankly, the talk about 'more family time'—very briefly—was not very convincing."[21]

The Salwens also took some heat on their own website, thepowerofhalf.com. There, a commenter identified as D. brings up the question of motivation: "If you want to have [an] interesting philosophical debate sometime, ask yourself (and your family) if there is any true unselfish altruism? Or if everyone is motivated by something . . . guilt, fear of god, wanting to impress others, voyeurism of others, joy, etc. Then when you are done, and you only have the clothes on your back and you are walking in the footsteps of Gandhi, please write another book."[22]

Sparring

Negative respiration can also take the form of serious and forthright criticism between competing experts or idea entrepreneurs operating in the same idea space.

Cesar Millan, for example, has the distinction of being the subject of a critical website called "Beyond Cesar Millan."[23] He has also come under attack by members of the veterinary and dog training community, the academic and established figures who have always questioned him.

One of his most vocal critics is Dr. Nicholas Dodman. He is a veterinary behaviorist, board certified by the American College of Veterinary Anesthesiologists and the American College of Veterinary Behaviorists, as well as a professor at Cummings School of

Veterinary Medicine at Tufts and program director of its Animal Behavior Clinic.

Dodman is also something of an idea entrepreneur himself. He is the author of many books, including *The Dog Who Loved Too Much: Tales, Treatments, and the Psychology of Dogs* (Bantam, 1997) and a number of scholarly articles, and is a speaker and worker of the ideaplex. He is a partner in a private for-profit enterprise, Pet Docs Inc. Among its many stated goals is to "consult for commercial producers of pet-related products."[24]

Dodman disapproves of Millan's methods to the point that he contends that the National Geographic Channel's series *The Dog Whisperer* has "put dog training back twenty years."[25]

But the debate is not as clear-cut as established academician versus instinctive practitioner. Dodman focuses on the "pharmacologic control of animal behavior problems" and, according to various sources, has a long history of treating dog problems with human-style medications, particularly antidepressants.[26]

Millan was almost certainly referring to the Dodman approach when he talked with me about veterinarians who have to give dogs injections in order to examine them. "I don't do that," he said. "By understanding how to gain their trust, the dog calms down."

Serious debate is useful respiration that helps clarify positions, further define ideas, and bring the idea to new audiences. Even as Dr. Dodman berates Millan, he includes him in the conversation.

LISTENING

It is entirely possible for the idea entrepreneur to follow the paths of respiration I have so far described—creating a set of mutually animating expressions, maintaining a current presence, and even engaging directly with immediate audiences—but not to *listen* to what others are saying about him, his expression, or the idea. Instead, he or she sees these engagements as so many opportunities to expound, to further press the idea into the minds of others, to refine the expressions. You have perhaps witnessed this phenomenon as well: I'm talking about the author who, in an interview, responds to a question with a set speech, or the speaker in a public forum who, when challenged, tries to persuade the questioner or prove her wrong.

The problems with not listening are many, but two stand out. The first is that, in order to fully apprehend an idea, people need to engage in dialogue, have a two-way (or multiway) exchange. They need to be able to ask questions, seek clarification, customize the idea to their particular circumstance—to see how their version of the idea sounds when *they* say it aloud. An idea cannot have influence, cannot be handed on, if it is not fully and personally understood.

Just as important, the idea entrepreneur needs to breathe in what others have to say in order to continue to animate the idea, to strengthen the expressions, keep them current, accumulate more material, and find new insights. This does not happen by lecturing.

Roger Nierenberg learned this very powerfully during one session of his special event called The Music Paradigm.

Classical Path

Nierenberg is a particularly intriguing example in this regard. He is the creator of a live program called the Music Paradigm, and its animating idea is that the group dynamics and leadership skills that make for a successful symphony orchestra are precisely those that can improve other kinds of organizations, such as businesses, not-for-profits, and government agencies.

The Music Paradigm is a combination of a talk, a live music performance, and a demonstration that puts the audience in the midst of the expression as it is being created. The program, which runs about two hours, features a symphony orchestra of as many as sixty-five professional players—hired especially for the occasion—with Maestro Nierenberg on the podium. The audience members seat themselves in chairs that have been placed among the sections of the orchestra—managers cheek-by-jowl with cellists, executives side by side with bassoonists. The audience becomes part of the orchestral "organization" and can observe and engage in the dynamics of performing together.

Nierenberg leads the group—orchestra and audience—through a series of exercises that involve the orchestra playing sections of a classical work in response to Nierenberg's leadership. Not only is it quite an experience to sit in the middle of an orchestra as it plays at full volume, the variations in the quality of the performance that result from Nierenberg's experiments are striking. As his website describes, the exercises "demonstrate basic and important truths about the functioning of an organization."[27]

Nierenberg has been leading sessions of the Music Paradigm since 1995 for many kinds of organizations in locations around the world, and the ideaplex has taken notice. In 1997, Nierenberg, working with the London Philharmonic Orchestra, was featured on the BBC television show *The Money Programme*. In 2001, the *New York Times* featured him in an article titled, "Allegro, Andante, Adagio and Corporate Harmony; A Conductor Draws Management Metaphors from Musical Teamwork." It ends with the story of one attendee who resolved to use a baton, instead of a croquet mallet, in his role as an executive—to work with a "lighter touch."[28]

The Music Paradigm became so successful that, in 2004, Nierenberg left his post with the Stamford orchestra to focus on it full time. He published a book based on the program, called *Maestro: A Surprising Story About Leading by Listening* (Portfolio, 2009). In 2011 alone, he led some fifty sessions in cities throughout the

United States as well as in Spain, the Netherlands, the Czech Republic, and Switzerland.

I have worked with Nierenberg at various points in his path to idea entrepreneurship, advising him on his book efforts, and traveling to see him conduct orchestras and lead the Music Paradigm in Stamford, New York, Boston, Prague, Stockholm, and Helsinki. Anna and I also interviewed him in his apartment in New York for this book.

The Oboe Line

Nierenberg did not set out to be an idea entrepreneur. His fascination is classical music and his education and training both led him toward a traditional career in music. He earned his BA in music from Princeton, a postgraduate degree in conducting at the Mannes College of Music (part of the New School in New York City), and a Master of Music from the Julliard School. He set off on a more-or-less standard path for a conductor, leading a chorale and eventually holding positions with two symphony orchestras— as music director of Connecticut's Stamford Symphony Orchestra and director of the Jacksonville Symphony Orchestra in Florida.

As he was building a successful career in this rarefied profession, however, Nierenberg felt there was something more he needed to do. People simply did not *get* classical music the way he did, were not as transported by it, as fascinated by it, as he was. They almost seemed unable to listen to it.

Nierenberg, in his role as conductor, also came to the realization that he was as fascinated by the *process* of conducting as much as he was by the music itself. How is it that one person, equipped at most with a baton (sometimes only hands), can evince from a group of musicians a performance of such dynamism and meaning that it evokes an emotional response from an audience? What does a conductor actually do? Nierenberg began to think beyond music, and consider conducting as a form of leadership. Might that be the different context within which people could better hear and understand classical music?

This thinking was sparked by a revelation Nierenberg had in the early 1980s, when he attended a performance of *Amadeus* on Broadway. The play, written by Peter Shaffer, is about the relationship between Wolfgang Amadeus Mozart and Antonio Salieri, a Mozart contemporary and also a composer, although of far lesser skill and renown. In one scene, Salieri listens to Mozart's Serenade Number 10, also known as the *Gran Partita,* a work for a woodwind and brass ensemble. Salieri has read through the score but is not prepared for the experience of actually listening to a performance, especially a passage for the oboe. "Salieri describes the oboe line," Nierenberg told us, "and describes his ecstasy at hearing this thing that he had never imagined before."

This struck him deeply. "The play had a way of creating context in which the music was more beautiful," he told us. "I wanted to create the context in which that experience can happen for other people."

The result, almost a decade later, was the Music Paradigm.

The Wrong Question

I asked Nierenberg what, if anything, *he* learned from conducting his sessions. Did he see the engagements as exercises in listening as much as in expressing his own idea?

He said that he looks forward to his sessions precisely because he does not know who his audience will be, how they will react, or what he will learn from them. He did a program for members of the National Automobile Auction Association, for example, essentially used-car redistributors and salespeople. As he was preparing for the engagement, Nierenberg said he was wondering, "Oh my God, what are they going to think of this Mendelssohn symphony? And just before they came in, I thought, I don't know whether this is going to work." To understand his audience he listened carefully to their comments and questions. "You have to find out who the people are," he said, "and play with them." In the end, the session worked "splendidly."

There is always a delicate balance in the room. In most sessions, Nierenberg achieves a feeling of openness and receptiveness, largely because he listens carefully and responds perceptively. The importance of doing so was brought home to Nierenberg at a session in Wellington, New Zealand, that proved to be a revelation for him.

The topic of the day was alignment. "We talk about how there are right angles in the way people play," Nierenberg said, "and about how the alignment of the body to the instrument, and the way the instrument plays, is critical." To kick off the discussion, he asked the audience members to observe the musicians near them as they played, looking for manifestations of alignment between body and instrument—right angles and parallel lines.

Nierenberg sometimes calls on people rather than waiting for volunteers to answer. In this session, he posed the question to an audience member who had not raised his hand. Unfortunately, the person could not come up with any examples of alignment as manifested in the angles of violin bows or bassoons. "He got very self-conscious," Nierenberg said. Finally, "I had to tell him the right answer." The atmosphere in the room changed. The audience could see that correct answers were expected and, since classical music was hardly their area of expertise, there was opportunity for embarrassment, failure, and being wrong. Although the session proceeded well enough and received praise at the end, Nierenberg knew that it could have been better.

Nierenberg was so upset by the session that he spent an hour reviewing every mistake that he might have made, the lessons he had learned, and writing them all down. "I learned that you never ask a closed question, you ask an open question," he said. Rather than ask, "Did you see right angles and parallel lines and where?" the question should be "What did you see?" This is a fundamental shift in live engagement, from the one who wishes to deliver an idea to the one who is helping a group consider that idea. It's as if to say: *I'm trying to understand the idea, to figure this out, along with you.* (Eckhart Tolle is a master at this.)

One goal of the Music Paradigm is to help people feel comfortable with content (the practices of classical music) that is unfamiliar to them. It takes a good deal of emotional intelligence on the part of the idea entrepreneur to enable people to have a new experience and feel safe enough to fully participate in discussion about it.

Surreptitious Intent

When Roger invented the Music Paradigm, he did so to create a context that would help people experience classical music, but in a "surreptitious" way—that is, within the context of a business setting with a clearly defined business goal. He would not announce to his clients that his goal was to further the cause of classical music, but rather to enlist classical music in the cause of organizational improvement.

However, the more Nierenberg listened to his audiences (he also survived a life-threatening illness along the way, and that may have emboldened him), the more he understood that almost everyone—including used-car salespeople—could respond to the music itself, and he freed himself enough so that he now can reveal his fascination more openly. No longer is his intent surreptitious, no more does he bend his narrative away from the feelings he really wants others to experience. "I always announce it now at the end of a session," he told Anna and me. Yes, he tells his audiences, he loves doing what he does, but helping their businesses is not his main objective. "My real agenda is that I'll feel successful if a lot of you now want to go to concerts," he confesses to them. As he said to us: "The fact that the Music Paradigm helps businesses—and I know it does—that's great and that's what pays me. But that's not what really drives me."

As Nierenberg learned, listening is not only a way to engage an audience so they will pay better attention, it is also a way to explore, enrich, and free *yourself*.

EVALUATION

With Nierenberg's revelation in mind, there is another important aspect of respiration that must be taken into consideration: its effect on you personally. It is impossible to create a sacred expression, take it public, attempt to break out, experience respiration, and suffer backlash without the whole endeavor having an effect on you. Feelings are handed *back* to you. Your own thinking is infected. The experience influences how you think and behave.

It would be tempting to think that you can stand a bit to the side, watching the ideaplex as it does whatever it does, and as people create their own expressions around your idea. But, depending on what your expectations are, if very little respiration occurs, you may feel profound disappointment—*the world has rejected me*. This feeling may be followed by resignation and, quite often, a renewed determination to keep accumulating and, one day, go public again.

Even if tremendous respiration takes place and your idea gains a widespread audience and influence, there can still be a risk. You may no longer have the inclination or time to engage in conversation or connect with the immediate audience, or keep up a current presence in any way, with the result that the idea loses its currency and elasticity and becomes less relevant.

Or you can become so overwhelmed by the demand for the idea and for you in particular, that you try to do too much, spread yourself too thin, cease to accumulate, and create so many expressions that they lose distinctiveness and the personal narrative gets lost.

A Blur

By September of 2011, when Anna and I talked with Hannah Salwen, she was mulling over her experience with the ideaplex. She had spent the summer thinking about her adventures and asking herself: "Did I actually just go through that? Did that really all just happen to me? Because it really did feel like a blur," she said. "And in some ways, I am upset about that."

What was upsetting to her? For one thing, because of the Power of Half project, Hannah had not experienced what she thought of as a "normal high school experience." She discovered, to her dismay, that some of her classmates did not appreciate her fame or her activism. "A lot of people hated the fact that I went to their school," she told us.

Some kids speculated that the Salwens had cooked up the whole project just to provide material for Hannah's senior speech—a talk that every graduating student is required to give before the entire student body. It would also make for a great college admissions essay, some doubters figured. "When people started saying this must have been some type of plan to get you guys famous or to get you into college, it was honestly shocking to me," Hannah told us. "When I was fourteen, I was not thinking about college at all. I was just thinking, like every other fourteen-year-old, this world is unfair. It was never about getting famous. It was never about getting into college." To add injury to insult, one of those classmates who doubted her turned out to be her boyfriend, who—along with his entire family, with whom she had been close—turned against her.

Still, Hannah is an upbeat and forthright young woman. It seemed to me that she had not allowed the downsides of the experience to overshadow the positive aspects. After all, *they had done it.* They had set a goal and achieved it. They had expressed an idea and taken it public. The Africa project itself was going well and that was, after all, the original intention. As I mentioned, the Salwens had also helped to start another charitable initiative, the Power of Half Schools, partly to respond to criticism that they should be focusing on people in the United States. It's a program to help kids in Atlanta who are "growing up on the other side of the opportunity divide, usually without a dad present, often in poverty," as Kevin writes in his blog on thepowerofhalf.com. "Our goal: To help them recognize that they have the power to become givers and they have resources the world needs them to give."[29]

What's more, the Salwens had inspired others to give back in their own way, which they knew from the e-mails and comments they received as well as the personal connections they made at events and engagements.

So, Hannah's doubts weren't so much about whether it had been a good idea to sell the family home, or whether they had realized their original goal of helping others, as it was about the nature of the ideaplex itself. It had been natural for Hannah to assume, especially at such an early age, that other people would be happy for the Salwens when they got on the *Today* show, published the book, and went on the speaking circuit. But Hannah is now well aware that it was the going public part that got the Salwens into hot water with some of their friends.

"How did our idea get so big?" she mused. "It was just because we decided, at one point, we need to go public with this because this could empower someone else to do a project. This has the power to inspire maybe one person to spend half the time they do watching TV and go volunteer somewhere, something as small as that."

Even though, when we met her, Hannah had enrolled in the nursing program at NYU, she was not entirely sure she would eventually become a nurse or what she might do, or where she might live, after she graduated. I asked her if—given all the issues involved with the family project, the experience of going public, the conflicts with friends, and the blur of the experience in the ideaplex—she would write another book.

"No."

Or at least, that's what Hannah said at the time. But almost a year later, we were in touch with her again. She had left the nursing program and was now at the Gallatin School, within NYU, which enabled her to create her own major—film and business. For her, *The Power of Half* may eventually look like a life experiment, an element of accumulation, and her sacred expression may be yet to come.

When we asked Hannah about her audience, she had said it was meant for well-to-do parents who could probably give more. But, on further consideration, Hannah said she intended something else too and had another audience in mind. When they first got started on the project, she said, "We had no idea that the real thing here was power." But she had come to realize that "the real thing was getting yourself empowered."

ULTIMATE AUDIENCE

Which brings me to the mention of one other audience, the most important of all, that I have so far neglected to mention—you.

I have been involved with many people as they considered the prospect of idea entrepreneurship, or were in the process of creating an expression, such as a book or a talk or a blog, and who tell themselves that they must relentlessly focus on identifying and knowing their "target" audiences.

That's important, but to not aim at yourself would be to risk missing every other potential audience.

The reason for this is that everybody who comes into contact with you or your expressions will know, instinctively and viscerally, if you have a genuine connection with your own idea and the associated material, including the practices. If they sense you do not have that connection, they will have less, possibly zero, interest. Without you as the one who breathes of the idea most deeply, as the most enthusiastic creator of respiration, no one else will draw a breath in its direction.

The second reason is that idea entrepreneurship is a risky business. There is absolutely no guarantee that the would-be idea entrepreneur will create a hit expression, reach multiple audiences, break out, build influence, or affect how people think and behave. There is always the possibility that almost nothing, at least nothing you hoped for or expected, will happen as the result of your efforts. But, if you have deeply connected with your own fascination, related your personal narrative in a way that enlightens you, and developed practices that have improved your own life, you still come out ahead.

If you do not fascinate yourself, you cannot fascinate others. Only if you fascinate others, develop a platform, and create respiration will you have a chance to take the next step of idea entrepreneurship: the creation of an enterprise.

5

ENTERPRISE

With successful respiration comes an intriguing opportunity: to create an idea-driven enterprise around you and your idea.

The enterprise may be a relatively simple organization whose main purpose is to support and leverage your time and energy. But, over time, it may grow into a more complex structure that comprises many parts and engages in many activities, not all of which you participate in. The idea-driven enterprise may even be created not only to extend activities beyond your involvement, but also to transcend you, such that it can last beyond your lifetime and even for generations. Given the newness of the phenomenon, however, these enterprises are still rare.

STRUCTURES

This enterprise-building impulse is perhaps the one that most distinguishes the emerging twenty-first-century version of the idea entrepreneur from its nineteenth-century prototype (e.g., Thoreau) and even the late twentieth-century version (e.g., Tolle).

Tim Ferriss, for example, seems to have instantly grasped the possibilities of the idea-driven enterprise and gone for it so intentionally and with such vigor that his endeavor could almost be termed a "pop-up" idea entrepreneurship—appearing, fully formed, as if overnight. Ferriss is the boy wonder (born 1977) advocate of the "four-hour" approach to what he calls "lifestyle design." His best-selling book, *The 4-Hour Workweek: Escape 9–5, Live Anywhere, and Join the New Rich* (Random House, 2007; nearly eight hundred thousand copies sold in the United States), argues, among other things, that you should get others to do everything you don't want to do. His follow-up book, *The 4-Hour Body: An Uncommon Guide to Rapid Fat-Loss, Incredible Sex, and Becoming Superhuman* (Random House, 2010; nearly four hundred thousand copies sold), shows how you can realize your body's full and amazing potential much faster than you might have imagined.

Not for Ferriss the slow accumulation and patient waiting for his moment. He seems to have no hesitation in revealing his many fascinations and has created a wildly amped-up version of the personal narrative (in the body book, most of the experiments with physicality and sexuality feature him) and has excelled in creating expressions that hand on his feelings. His work is highly practical, replete with methods and experiments and how-to's. His immediate audience is largely composed of young men, particularly those in their twenties, who have, in turn, brought the Ferriss plan to their younger brothers, as well as their fathers and uncles—with mothers, girlfriends, sisters, and female friends pulled in (one way or another) as well.

Ferriss is exquisitely aware of the idea entrepreneurship model and diligently commits to it, such that, in 2008, Wired.com named him the Greatest Self-Promoter of All Time, based on a reader poll.[1] Ferriss built a mutually reinforcing platform of expressions with extraordinary alacrity, combining the successful books with speaking engagements and events, and a lively current presence, including a blog as well as merchandise recommendations. On his website, Ferriss makes the following claim: "Since his debut presentation on *The 4-Hour Workweek* at the world-famous SXSW Interactive conference on March 12, 2007, Tim has been invited to speak at some of the most innovative companies and universities in the world, ranging from Google and PayPal to Princeton University, the Wharton School, and the Stanford Graduate School of Business. He has also been invited to speak and keynote at world-renowned technology summits including Supernova, FOO Camp, Community Next, and the Web 2.0 Exposition, where he shared the stage with figures like Eric Schmidt, chairman of the board of Google, and Jeff Bezos, founder and CEO of Amazon."[2]

Ferriss's facility with the model is so complete that he has distinguished himself as a would-be guru's guru, a meta-idea entrepreneur who not only practices the model, but also teaches some of its methods. For example, so many people wanted to know how he had achieved such incredible respiration (although they probably didn't call it that), Ferriss created a weekend retreat that promised to reveal the secrets of exactly how he went about making his books into monster best-sellers and how others could do the same. Cost for the three-day session was $10,000, not including flights and hotel, and enrollment was limited to two hundred people.[3] That would have brought in some $2 million of gross revenue, if all the spots were taken. That is very canny, and cheeky, working of the ideaplex.

Demand

Not every idea entrepreneur is so consumed by the phenomenon itself, but still, the ideaplex is so vast and the demand for content so huge that an almost overwhelming number of opportunities may become available: invitations to appear at interesting conferences in exotic locations; possibilities for partnerships with intriguing organizations and celebrated people; requests for interviews, guest blog posts, and articles; consultations and special events; hook-ups and tie-ins and spin-offs galore.

One response is to try to manage it all by yourself, sometimes with the help of an assistant (who might also be one's life partner), and usually with a team of trusted advisers, such as a lawyer, accountant, agent, media consultant, and others.

With a self-centric organization, you may find yourself working like a maniac, devoting your every waking moment to the effort. If you don't burn out, you can sustain the activity for long periods of time, even an entire career. Mireille Guiliano, for example, has no full-time help. Roger Nierenberg has employed as many as three people, but worked on his own for many years. Edward Tufte continues to be active, even though he only occasionally causes a new gust of respiration, as he did when, in 2010, President Obama appointed him to serve on the Recovery Independent Advisory Panel. "The panel's mission," as stated on its website, "is to recommend ways to the Recovery Board to find and prevent fraud, waste, and abuse in the Recovery program."[4] He is quoted on the site as saying: "I'm doing this because I like accountability and transparency, and I believe in public service. And it is the complete opposite of everything else I do. Maybe I'll learn something."[5] In other words, Tufte is still accumulating.

The self-centric approach can, of course, put a tremendous strain on idea entrepreneurs and can wreak havoc with their personal lives. When I asked Cesar Millan about the stresses involved in his life, he put it this way: "To be what I am, you have to go through a lot of downs. You have to go through all of it." What was his worst down? He hesitated a moment. Why should he reveal his down moments to me?

"My divorce," he said at last. Ilusion and Cesar had been married in 1994 and had two sons together, and she had been a longtime partner in his enterprise. Then, in 2010, she had had enough. "I was in England, giving a seminar. I was changing the world," he told Anna and me. "Then, boom, my world was changed in a phone call." Millan was shocked; he did not see it coming. In the next few months, he lost forty pounds. "That just tells you how much stress I had emotionally, psychologically," he said. It came out only later (and he did not mention it to us in our interview) that this particular down was so bad that Millan had attempted suicide.[6]

Not every self-centric idea entrepreneur, however, takes the do-it-all approach. Instead, they carefully pick and choose among the opportunities, to try to maintain some kind of balance and control. These idea entrepreneurs will take on projects and activities to the limit of their capabilities and interest, but they are not inclined to create or sanction the building of large enterprises, to license or franchise themselves, or maintain a current presence just for the sake of doing so.

Trying to Say No

Mireille Guiliano has had her difficulties with juggling so much activity and trying to maintain some kind of equilibrium and control, while also responding to requests, maintaining a current presence, and developing new expressions.

In the spring of 2011, I asked in an e-mail what was next for her. "Next is 'not written in stone,'" she replied. She wrote that she had submitted four ideas for books to her agent, who had liked them all and she had been constantly involved in activities associated with her previous two books throughout the previous year. She does not think of these activities as "promotional" but rather as ways to share ideas, tell stories, gather content, and connect with and help people. Now she was "hoping for a short sabbatical!"

Guiliano also does a good deal of mentoring "both via e-mail and meetings (time-consuming but rewarding)." She had been advising one mentee for many years, helping her think about her career, and the woman had received a promotion that involved a move to Paris, which had been the "dream of her life." Guiliano invited her to visit during her summer stay in Provence, during which time she planned to "host a dinner for her inviting a dozen or so French friends who can always be of help during her stay (I believe in networking)."

In addition to all of this, Guiliano continues to write pieces for print and online content venues, when it doesn't interfere with book writing. She also travels extensively. She was headed to Japan, where her business book, *Women, Work, and the Art of Savoir Faire*, had gotten a lot of attention, and *French Women Don't Get Fat* was "still in people's mind especially with more Japanese women going to work and having less time to cook."

From January through May of 2011, she had been traveling and promoting her ideas—through press interviews, lectures, and as a guest mentor for Education Without Borders—and had visited Beijing, Tokyo, Amsterdam, Paris, Dubai, and Abu Dhabi.

On and on she went. She was participating in an online discussion group about current issues related to France, and had appeared on French television and in a documentary by a German filmmaker. "And last but not least," she wrote, she had been "maintaining my web sites/facebook/twitter and answering daily fan mail from all over the world." That, she admitted, "takes quite a bit of time though I have 2 part timers helping." Although she had not intended to make idea entrepreneurship a full-time job, Guiliano was "still trying to learn to say no."

Some idea entrepreneurs, however, want to do much more than their personal energies will allow, and decide they need help in managing it all. These people—like Eckhart Tolle, Al Gore, and, more recently, Cesar Millan—have to let go a bit, embrace ideas that come from others, and allow themselves to be managed to some degree.

When the endeavor starts to grow, however, new issues—managing people and structuring the organization—arise and start to consume the energy of the idea entrepreneur. The challenge is to keep the idea foremost, the respiration going, not to confuse or corrupt the personal narrative and, very important, to prevent the organization from becoming more important than the idea itself.

Which brings us to the topic of money, without which no such organization can survive.

REVENUE

So far, I have not talked much about revenue for the simple reason that moneymaking and profit taking are not the primary goals of the idea entrepreneur, but revenue is of course essential to sustaining the individual and then building an enterprise.

Revenue can also present some difficulties for the idea entrepreneur. The most important is that there can seem to be a conflict of motives when too much money is involved. Is this person pursuing an idea with the goal of making a difference, starting a movement, changing the world in some way that is life-affirming and meant to lead to a larger social good? Or is the guy really just trying to make money for himself?

Idea entrepreneurs whose enterprises grow very large and bring in millions, even tens of millions of dollars, have to be mindful of how they earn their revenue, how they spend it, and how they behave in relation to money. Thoreau and Emerson did not have this problem; both struggled with money throughout their lives. Mireille Guiliano and Edward Tufte have made millions, but they're still personally engaged and have not tried to leverage their resources to overinflate their efforts. The endeavors of Eckhart Tolle, Deepak Chopra, Stephen Covey, and others, by contrast, have grown into large organizations that bring in so much money their leaders start to look more like impresarios—or worse, like hucksters—and less like idea entrepreneurs.

Omnivorous

As the most trenchant example of this phenomenon I offer Martha Stewart, who began as an idea entrepreneur but is now a personal brand and leader of a commercial empire. Although Martha, the iconic character, remains at the center of the enterprise, Martha, the human being, has become something else. She is at the head of a very large profit-making organization—Martha Stewart Living Omnimedia (MSLO)—and yet she still is exploring her fascination and modeling her idea through practices, and causing plenty of respiration, both positive and negative, along the way.

Stewart started out as an idea entrepreneur very much like the others we have discussed. She had a genuine fascination: the art of entertaining and the home. It connected with a fundamental human concern: the role of women and the nature of social relationships. She had a compelling personal narrative that intertwined with the idea: her early marriage; her brief employment as a stockbroker; fixing up an old farmhouse; starting a catering company; writing articles for various publications, including

House Beautiful and the *New York Times* Lifestyle section; and going public with her first book, *Entertaining* (Clarkson Potter, 1982), which became a best-seller.

Entertaining opened the door to idea entrepreneurship for Stewart. She talked about the success of the book in an interview with *CosmoGirl* magazine: "[E]ven though it was an accomplishment and I got asked to do speaking engagements all over the country, I realized that there was so much more to do. I decided to work really hard and write one book a year. Then I started to think, Gosh, I have many more ideas than one book a year. I started the monthly magazine *Martha Stewart Living* so that I could get more people to work with me to portray all of the beautiful how-to ideas that I had."[7]

Stewart not only had the will to create an enterprise, she also experienced a remarkable convergence with the zeitgeist. Her central idea—that a beautiful home life and a busy, successful professional life are not mutually exclusive—coincided with the issues that American women were dealing with in the 1980s and '90s. The feminist movement of the 1960s and '70s had achieved enormous advancements by that time; the number of women in the workforce—particularly mothers, and women working full time—had nearly doubled since the start of the movement, and pay equity had also risen. Yet women were facing a new identity crisis: if they were now defined by their education and careers, who were they at home?

Stewart has successfully maintained a current presence and continued to connect with the zeitgeist for more than thirty years. Her fascination and central idea have not changed, but her content and expressions have evolved to reflect and respond to what women are looking for in their home lives. Martha is her idea; the idea is Martha. Her face is her emblem; her life is her sacred expression.

Today, Stewart is nonexecutive chairman of Martha Stewart Living Omnimedia, a public company that in 2011 had nearly six hundred employees and total revenue of over $221 million.[8] The company has a massive mutually animating platform of expressions, in three main areas: publishing, broadcasting, and merchandising. Even with all of that organizational size and considerable revenue, it's difficult to kick Stewart out of the pantheon of idea entrepreneurs and into the role of corporate executive. One reason for this is her experience with money. Not only did it get her in trouble, it added an episode to her personal narrative that proved both iconic and revelatory.

In 2001, Stewart was indicted for insider trading and was forced to resign as chair and CEO of MSLO. In 2004, she was convicted on all charges brought against her of conspiracy and obstruction and sentenced to five months in prison, followed by five months of home confinement. She resigned as CEO of her company and production of her television show was suspended.

What effect would jail time have on Stewart? Would she be revealed as the brittle phony that some people suspected she really was beneath the smiling exterior? Although I was not inside with her, the story is that she lived out her term as if it were a renewed period of accumulation. She did not give up on her fascination, continued to express herself, and adapted her practices for the prison environment. She offered to cook for inmates and ran a yoga class for them. She posted a Christmas message calling for penal reform and criticizing prison food. She lost ten pounds, arranged flowers, raked leaves, cleaned, and crocheted.[9] Granted, Stewart was doing time at the Federal Prison Camp in Alderson, West Virginia, which, while remote and not where she asked to be sent, is hardly on par with Alcatraz. Stewart did no time in solitary and busted no rock, but it would be impossible not to characterize her period in jail as one of hardship, which she endured with grace and emerged from stronger than before.

Still, that period in Stewart's narrative can also be seen as a turn-ing point from individual idea entrepreneurship to a branded enter-prise, a time in which money had become so important to her that she had gotten involved in illegal activities to make more of it.

After much consideration of Martha Stewart, and discussion about her with many friends and colleagues, I'd have to put her in a special category—where Steve Jobs might also reside—of idea entrepreneurs whose narrative and idea seem to remain genuine, even as commercial empires and myths grow around them.

Streams

But let us set aside the special cases to consider the typical revenue streams of the idea entrepreneur.

The main stream usually derives from the sale of expressions, including books and other writings, admission fees to talks and special events, speaking fees, and various forms of reproductions of the expressions, including audiotapes, DVDs, and downloads of the talks and events.

Some idea entrepreneurs take in revenue from other kinds of merchandise, but are careful to keep the selection small and very closely related to the practices. Edward Tufte offers pads of paper (at $10 each) as well as fine art prints. Cesar Millan sells a collar and lead, a stain remover, and other dog-related items. From Eckhart Tolle, one can buy cards, calendars, and CDs of music that helps in creating stillness and quieting the mind.

The idea entrepreneur may also sell a limited amount of adver-tising for services or merchandise offered by partners, advocates, or sponsors. Millan, for example, includes links to sponsors who are commercial providers of dog medicines and products. (More complexity in the Millan-Dodman debate!)

Some idea entrepreneurs consult—that is, get actively involved with clients on how to solve a particular problem or how to put the practices to work in a specific situation—but they tend to leave that activity behind as the other sources of revenue increase. That's because each consulting engagement is different and customized, tends to involve a fair amount of time, and requires that the idea entrepreneur act as a service provider as opposed to as a motivator. Moreover, anything short of superb results can cast doubt upon the idea, the framework, and the efficacy of the practices.

These are some of the reasons Cesar Millan stopped making house calls and why Edward Tufte gave up his consulting activities. In an article titled "Sermon on the Mountain: How Edward Tufte Led Bose Out of the Land of Chartjunk," writer James Surowiecki, author of *The Wisdom of Crowds* (Doubleday, 2004), describes some of Tufte's adventures in consulting. In it, Tufte claims that he has, over the years, consulted for many large companies, including technology leaders such as IBM, but that he no longer takes on many such assignments because consulting involves "too big an effort for too small a result." That is especially true when dealing with very large enterprises, as Tufte often did. "Trying to change IBM is like trying to change Sweden," Tufte is quoted as saying in Surowiecki's article.[10]

Books

Despite a popular conception that it's difficult to make money on books, and despite industry infighting over who will set prices and even the deep discounting of the online retailers, the book is still often the largest and most important source of revenue for the idea entrepreneur—especially at the beginning.

Although the economics of book revenue are a little complicated and a bit bizarre, idea entrepreneurs including Cesar Millan, Eckhart Tolle, Mireille Guiliano, Stephen Covey, Tim Ferriss,

Martha Stewart, and many others have sold millions of copies of their books and reaped millions of dollars in revenue from those sales. Cesar Millan's books have sold nearly two million copies in the United States, translating to substantial revenue for both the publisher and Millan.

Although I would not call Barack Obama an idea entrepreneur (though he might well become one after he leaves the presidency), he offers an interesting example of how important the success of a book, and the amount of revenue it generates, can be to creating a platform.

In 1991, Obama graduated from Harvard Law School at the age of thirty. In 1995 he published his first book, *Dreams from My Father,* for which he had received a small but not insignificant advance in the range of $30,000.[11] The publisher is reported to have printed twenty thousand copies, a fairly typical number for such a book,[12] and some eight to nine thousand hardcover copies were sold.[13]

The book created enough respiration that it likely helped Obama win a seat in the Illinois state senate in 1996, where he served until he ran for the nomination as U.S. senator for Illinois, which he won in March 2004. Just about four months later, on July 27, 2004, Obama delivered the speech at the Democratic National Convention that thrust him onto the national stage. Random House, sensing that this was a guy who knew his way around the ideaplex, leaped on the opportunity and re-released *Dreams from My Father* that August. It sold briskly, selling an average of three to five thousand copies every week for the next several weeks. That November, Obama won the race and became senator.

A memoir may be a sacred expression of the author's personal narrative, but not so much of an idea or intellectual framework, so Obama felt he needed another book. He signed on with Robert Barnett, a big-time Washington-based lawyer and agent, and Barnett brokered a deal reputed to be worth about $1.9 million.[14] That's a monster advance, if not quite in the Bill Clinton league—he reportedly received in the range of $15 million for his memoir, *My Life*.[15]

The Audacity of Hope came out in October of 2006 and sold tens of thousands of copies right out of the gate. The sales no doubt helped him reach multiple audiences and further encouraged him to make a run for the presidency, which he announced in February 2007. By the end of that year, Obama reported that he had earned $4.1 million on sales of his books for that year.[16] The book revenues put Obama in the club of millionaire senators (some 47 percent of U.S. House and Senate members are estimated to be millionaires, as calculated by the Center for Responsive Politics[17]) and provided him with resources that made it easier to pursue the presidency. He no longer had to worry about earning a living.

In January and February of 2008, as Obama gradually took the lead in the Democratic race from Hillary Clinton, sales of Obama's books climbed to as many as thirty-five thousand copies per week. In November, Obama won the election and *Dreams from My Father* continued to sell at a rapid pace. On his tax returns for 2008, Obama reported royalties in the range of $2.5 million from his two books for 2008, out of $2.8 million total income for Barack and Michelle.[18] Based on the president's own accounting, and knowledge of the typical industry payment, Jeff Zeleny of the *New York Times* estimated that Obama had earned at least $8 million from his books, as of March 2009.[19]

Not only does Obama's story show that books can produce a good deal of revenue, it also demonstrates that the quality of the expression is important. Obama is hardly the only politician to publish a book as part of the process of striving for and gaining office. Almost every candidate in the 2012 presidential election campaign produced a book (including *Core of Conviction: My Story* by

Michele Bachmann; *This Is Herman Cain! My Journey to the White House* by Herman Cain; *Fed Up! Our Fight to Save America from Washington* by Rick Perry; *No Apology: The Case for American Greatness* by Mitt Romney; *A Nation Like No Other: Why American Exceptionalism Matters* by Newt Gingrich; and many others) but none of them achieved the respiration, generated the revenue, or had the impact that Obama's books did. Nor did any of them enable their authors to achieve their ultimate goal of becoming president.

Speaking and Special Events

A successful book, while an important source of revenue in itself, can also be the key that unlocks other revenue streams, particularly speaking engagements and special events, which can grow to be the more substantial source of income. Speaking engagements, as Emerson taught us, can also create respiration that increases the sale of books and other writings. Speaking further serves as a mechanism of accumulation, which facilitates the development of new expressions.

Speaking is an efficient source of revenue. Unlike a book, which can take years to produce and is fixed in form, a presentation can be developed much more rapidly, is easily adaptable to various situations, and, once developed, consumes only an hour or so (a day or two at most, in the case of a special event) to actually deliver. While they are flexible and adaptable, presentations can also be standardized and modularized, further aided by the use of PowerPoint and other media. I have seen idea entrepreneurs prepare an hour-long speech the night before, simply by shuffling segments and rearranging slides and clips.

Speaking engagements can deliver healthy fees, especially when calculated at an hourly rate. Even a relatively unknown idea entrepreneur, with a useful idea, a modest set of expressions, and respiration limited to an expert audience, can command fees of $2,000–$5,000 for an engagement that may involve a formal talk, a panel appearance, a workshop, and perhaps a breakfast and a dinner.

A more experienced speaker, with a well-known blog or a strongly selling book (and a mouth of chiseled beauty like Emerson's couldn't hurt), can earn $10,000–$25,000 per engagement and do perhaps fifteen to twenty-five events per year, which can amount to a half million dollars or more of annual revenue, with plenty of time left over for activities and the creation of new expressions.

Fees wander up into the stratosphere for superstars like Jim Collins, Bill Clinton, Al Gore, and Donald Trump (although I do not consider him an idea entrepreneur). According to several sources, Clinton's fee ranges from upwards of $100,000 to more than $400,000, and he made enough money from speaking in the years following his presidency to retire his considerable debts.[20] During the 2011 presidential primary race, candidate Mitt Romney, obviously aware of the going rates in the speaking market, admitted that he got speaker's fees "from time to time" but "not very much"—just $374,327 in the preceding year.[21]

The limitation of the speaking engagement, of course, is that it takes place in real time and there can be no substitutions. The idea entrepreneur cannot send along a surrogate in his place. And, if speaking is the major source of revenue, it dries up as soon as the idea entrepreneur retires, has to cancel, or dies.

Plus, as Emerson discovered, a heavy speaking schedule is wearying. That's why the idea entrepreneur with a wide enough audience turns to the special event as a more attractive, controllable, and reliable revenue source. Tufte has been conducting his one-day course for twenty years, and it continues to fill up, providing a revenue stream that is not only reliable but also flexible (he can adjust the number of dates to suit his schedule), more so than consulting gigs or paid speaking engagements, which can ebb and flow. Cesar Millan does one-man shows around the world, playing in stadium-sized venues.

These events produce revenue in themselves, and also provide new content for recordings and other packages. Eckhart Tolle's speaking engagements are available in an extensive array of audio and video forms, and he has been inventive in his creation of an online presence. In May of 2008, at the time of publication of *A New Earth: Awakening to Your Life's Purpose*, Tolle and Oprah Winfrey teamed up to conduct a ten-week webinar, with each new session focused on a single chapter of the book. The webinar has been accessed from Winfrey's website more than thirty-five million times as of 2009, and the book has sold some six million copies worldwide.[22]

Merchandise

I have mentioned the sale of related merchandise as one source of revenue for the idea entrepreneur, and that has been the model for many years. However, merchandise is now playing a new, larger, and more complicated role in the idea entrepreneur's enterprise: not only is it becoming more central, in some cases it can be seen as a form of expression and a key element of respiration. Merchandise is, after all, a form of exchange. If audience members choose to purchase a book, a ticket to a special event, a dog collar, a poster, or a brownie pan, they are engaging in an indirect conversation with the idea entrepreneur and following a practice.

So, if you have gained a good deal of influence and multiple audiences you can find yourself besieged with opportunities to develop products, endorse them, or brand them with your name.

Mireille Guiliano, for example, was taken aback at the number and kind of opportunities presented to her for creating merchandise by various would-be business partners. So far, she has said no to all of them. "I turned down so many offers and people told me I was stupid," she told us. "I could be a billionaire! Whether it was from a television show or making my own products, selling my own this or that. And I said, 'You don't understand. The world doesn't need another brownie mix, or a frying pan with my name on it.'"

Still, Guiliano admits to being tempted. Perhaps merchandise, properly managed, could provide the tools that would make it easier for Americans to put the French approach into practice? If someone proposed the idea of creating a set of small plates, for example, which would encourage eating smaller portions (an important tenet of the French lifestyle), she might be interested. Perhaps at Crate & Barrel or Williams-Sonoma, with illustrations that would appeal to young people. But, as with most idea entrepreneurs, she does not really see herself as a businessperson, even though she spent three decades as a corporate executive. She sees her mission as being education, not commerce.

BLURRED LINE

The connection between change-the-world ideas and profit-the-enterprise merchandise has grown stronger and stronger. At the same time, there has been a trend for profit-making companies to do more social good, not as an afterthought but as an activity central to their operations.

As the trends converge, a new form of idea entrepreneurship is emerging, in which the idea and product have equal weight. The idea is the company's strategy, rather than an afterthought or ancillary activity. The product is an expression of the idea, rather than a reflection of it. The leader of the company is an idea entrepreneur who is also a corporate executive.

One for One

An intriguing example is Blake Mycoskie, founder of TOMS, a company that makes slipper-like canvas shoes modeled on the *alpargata*—Argentine rope-soled shoes that are rather like the espadrille that comes from Catalonia. Blake's idea is summed up in the phrase "one for one," which essentially means that a company should share goods equally with those who need the product. So, for every pair of shoes sold by TOMS, the company gives a pair to a child who cannot afford shoes and who is at risk of foot-borne illnesses. Depending on the part of the world, these ailments include infection from worms in the soil (some 400 million children are either infected or at risk of infection in this way, according to TOMS) or from schistosomiasis, another worm-borne disease with a host of unpleasant and debilitating health consequences.[23]

Anna and I spoke with Mycoskie not long before the publication of his book, *Start Something That Matters* (Random House, 2011). He told us that the inspiration for TOMS (which is a shortening of the original name, Tomorrow's Shoes) came to him during a trip to Argentina in 2006, where he was struck by the number of children who ran around without shoes. That might have seemed a positive state of affairs, except that the kids were particularly susceptible to diseases transmitted through the soil. What's more, many of the shoeless kids were not allowed to attend school because they did not have proper attire.

Mycoskie decided start a company that would address the problem through his one-for-one model. The company was almost immediately successful. Less than a year after that first trip, Mycoskie returned to Argentina and distributed ten thousand pairs of shoes to kids in the region. Today the shoes retail for upwards of $45, and in 2010 the *Wall Street Journal* estimated that TOMS had generated $33 million in revenues since its founding.[24]

Mycoskie is quick to point out that he didn't start TOMS as a business, but as a project—in effect, a practice. Kids needed shoes. Mycoskie needed a solution. "I didn't start this to solve all the world's problems. I am a very linear, straightforward person and thinker. I saw kids who needed shoes and thought, 'Hey, I can help them.' We could keep these kids in shoes if we didn't approach it like a charity and made it a business. We could be more sustainable, more predictable."

So while Mycoskie runs a business, rather than runs with an idea, his enterprise shares characteristics with idea entrepreneurship. Other businesses exist that follow the model, such as Warby Parker, purveyor of eyeglasses, whose promise is "buy a pair, give a pair."[25] So perhaps one could argue that one for one is Mycoskie's idea and that his company, more than the product itself, is the sacred expression of that idea.

Like Tim Ferriss, a good deal of Mycoskie's success comes from his ability to understand and work the ideaplex. He already had quite a whirl there as a contestant in the second season of CBS's *The Amazing Race,* and had experiences from four previous start-ups when he launched TOMS. He even founded a 24/7 reality TV channel in 2002. Mycoskie understands that his personal narrative was crucial to the potential success of TOMS. "People don't get initially excited—especially in the media—about the concepts. They get excited about people," Mycoskie told us. "And I think that was really important for my story."

Mycoskie intends to stick with the one-for-one movement, and it's no longer just about shoes. In 2011, TOMS branched out and added a line of eyewear. For every pair of sunglasses sold, the company restores someone's sight by giving them prescription glasses, medical treatment, or surgery.

With the company's expansion and continued success, some serial entrepreneurs might be thinking about cashing out, but Mycoskie is not interested in exit strategies. "My idea is that you can help people and do well and earn a living together. I think the minute you would go public or the minute you would sell, anyone who would be interested purely on a financial basis probably wouldn't share the same values. And I would never want to take that risk with something as beautiful as what we've created."

So although Mycoskie's fascinations and motivations are a little different from those of other idea entrepreneurs, he is almost as mindful not to tip too far toward the bottom line—or to let an outsider change his fundamental idea—even as his merchandise offering grows. And his products, narrative, idea, and personal engagement are not at odds. They animate each other.

Mycoskie sees TOMS as "a movement, and a community." And, as it grows, he hopes that his endeavor "becomes more about the community and less about Blake as a person because that's more sustainable long term."

Hybrids

Other idea entrepreneurs create structures with similarities to Mycoskie's model, in that it is hard to distinguish the generation of revenue from the furthering of the idea. Some idea entrepreneurs have created hybrid organizations that have distinct but closely connected for-profit and not-for-profit components, with the profit-making unit pushing most of its revenue into the not-for-profit activities. This structure enables the for-profit unit of the enterprise to bring in money through commercial sales—and for the idea entrepreneur himself to take some profit—while the other unit can gather revenue and also accept charitable contributions.

These organizational structures can become quite complex and hard to disentangle, but they still look different from companies that are primarily for-profits even if they have a charitable entity, in two ways. First, the products or services they offer to generate income reflect the ideas, philosophy, or concepts of the idea entrepreneur himself. Second, the entity does not view profit as its main goal.

An example is Dr. Andrew Weil, an early advocate of the idea that the human body is its own best healer, who spoke with one of my research colleagues, John Landry. Weil believes that we should focus on health—strengthening the body's natural defense systems and supporting its healing powers—rather than focusing on disease and trying to fix the body when things go wrong. Like other prevention advocates, Weil urges good nutrition, the prudent use of vitamins, regular physical activity, and meditation and also favors herbs, acupuncture, and other nonconventional treatments (but only those that he calls "evidence-based") for various conditions. Above all, he argues for an integrative approach to medicine, combining conventional and alternative methods.

Although Weil had created a successful set of expressions, including the development of a university-based fellowship program to train physicians in integrative medicine, he wanted to secure a stable financial platform from which to continue the development of his ideas. To that end, he established the Weil Foundation, whose mission is "dedicated to supporting integrative medicine through training, education, and research."[26] Because it is a nonprofit, the Weil Foundation can accept charitable donations, but these are rarely enough. So Weil created a for-profit entity, Weil Lifestyle LLC, which judiciously licenses his name for a wide array of nutritional and skin care products, from plum tomatoes to face serums and vitamins. Many are developed by Weil Lifestyle with Weil's direct input, others are produced by outside companies with his endorsement. Weil says he contributes all after-tax profits from Weil Lifestyle LLC products to the Weil Foundation.[27]

In spite of his commercial success, Dr. Weil says he does not consider products his primary expression. Indeed, since our interview with him, he has continued to write and publish, and has focused on broadening his efforts in physician education through annual academic conferences on nutrition and health.

Multifaceted Enterprise

Eckhart Tolle's enterprise comprises a number of activities, structures, and units.

The original source of revenue for Tolle was *The Power of Now*, and books remain an important source of revenue for him and Kim Eng, his "life partner and associate."[28] But they went on to build a mutually animating platform of expressions and then created a multifaceted enterprise that thrives thanks to a variety of revenue streams: live events, online events, Eckhart Tolle TV, an online community, books, and merchandise. Not only do all of these elements produce revenue, they also serve as ways to accumulate more material, generate respiration, and inspire new expressions.

Events and engagements are a major activity. In addition to the talks, intensives, and retreats, in 2010 Tolle experimented with the big venue speaking tour, which made stops in Australia, Europe, and North America, including one at Madison Square Garden in New York.[29] Tolle, who is a rather shy and private person, seemed not to thrive on that kind of engagement, and thereafter reduced his schedule of live appearances. But all of that talking and eventing is captured so that it can be purchased or downloaded, for a price.

Perhaps Tolle's most intriguing activity—which serves triple duty as a form of expression, revenue stream, and mechanism for the accumulation of content is Eckhart Tolle TV, launched July 1, 2009. It is essentially a private TV network, delivered through the web, available on a subscription basis with new video content available each month. The site claims it has members from 130 countries.[30] Some segments are shot before a live audience in a studio setting, and members can pay a $150 admission fee to attend the taping.[31]

Television is not only a source of revenue, it is of course an effective generator of respiration. As one of the founders and executive producer Anthony McLaughlin explained it: "You can travel the world and teach 2,000 to 3,000 people at a time, but that's got limitations. The idea of the online model is to make it really affordable and be able to go worldwide on demand."[32]

Although the Tolle enterprise has been clever about creating sources of revenue, it also provides many free materials. On the website there are links to articles and interviews and a section called "Eckhart Likes," as well as videos, a newsletter, a curriculum, and other information. Also available, for free, are a variety of YouTube recordings of Tolle speaking and the online seminars Oprah Winfrey created with Tolle for her website. It's reported that 35 million people have visited Oprah's site to hear Tolle dispense his wisdom.[33]

Ken MacQueen, a reporter for *Maclean's* magazine, looked into the Tolle enterprise and wrote that Tolle "says he keeps his organization as small as possible, and yet his product lines and plans for global reach grow ever more ambitious." Tolle responded, "It's necessary for it to get out into the world, but one needs to be careful that the organization doesn't become self-serving."[34] Another writer, Cathy Lynn Grossman, describes in *USA Today* how Tolle reinvests his revenue from one expression into another, a practice that "enables him to reach an ever-widening audience without forcing solitude-loving Tolle to travel constantly."[35]

Tolle himself is aware of the doubts people have about the effect of revenue on the idea entrepreneur who purports to be about life affirmation rather than profit making. One question on his website's frequently asked questions page asks why Tolle charges a fee to attend his events. The response: "Eckhart would like to spread the teaching around the world at no cost. With a number of internal expenses including salaries, office space, rental fee for locations of events, airfare for Eckhart to travel to each destination etc., it is necessary to charge admission at lectures in order to continue to spread the message."[36]

CADENCE

The need to bring in revenue to cover the expenses of operating an enterprise can put pressure on the idea entrepreneur to create new expressions that will generate further revenue. This can have an effect on the cadence of production, by which I mean when and how often new elements are introduced to the platform and how they animate one another. Every idea entrepreneur has a different cadence, with different effects on respiration.

While some, like Edward Tufte, have maintained a rather measured and deliberate cadence (four major books, a "textbooklet," and an essay, since 1989), the pressure of the ideaplex and the opportunities for more and more activity tend to result more often in an ever-accelerating cadence. Deepak Chopra, for example, has created a cadence of activity that is remarkable in its extent and duration, although it started relatively slowly.

When Chopra published his first book, *Creating Health*, in 1987, it did not produce the kind of response that *French Women Don't*

Get Fat or *Power of Now* did, but did create some respiration and provided an opportunity for Chopra to start building a platform. It was not until 1994 that Chopra came out with the book that has become his sacred expression, *The Seven Spiritual Laws of Success: A Practical Guide to the Fulfillment of Your Dreams*. It became a best-seller, generated respiration far and wide, enabled Chopra to break out, fueled his speaking engagements, and filled up his spe-cial-event calendar.

Since then, Chopra has produced an astonishing flow of books, sometimes releasing as many as four new titles a year. In all, he has published some sixty-five books in the twenty-five years since *Creating Health* appeared. In these books he has sought to extend his ideas to a wide variety of audiences—teens, seniors, parents—and cover every possible endeavor, from weight loss to personal finance, to the point that you know he cannot possibly be writing all these books himself (many do have a coauthor), and you won-der if he can even keep track of them all. Some of them seem to reach the point of self-satire—with such titles as *The Seven Spir-itual Laws of the Superheroes, Golf for Enlightenment*, and *Perfect Digestion*.

Along with, and largely because of, this cadence, Chopra has successfully maintained a current presence. New profiles of him appear regularly, in *The Nation*, the *Boston Globe*, and elsewhere. He seems never to turn down a request to talk (although he prob-ably actually does turn down hundreds, if not thousands), has been interviewed on NPR and ABC News Radio, and at various times, for various purposes, has appeared on television shows ranging from *The Rosie O'Donnell Show* to *Larry King Live*.[37] He also has his own radio show, *Wellness Radio*, on Sirius. He writes a weekly column for the *San Francisco Chronicle*, frequently con-tributes to Oprah.com, and sometimes to the *Huffington Post* and the *Washington Post*.

Chopra continues to engage directly with his audiences. In recent years, he has participated in "evenings" with Deepak Chopra, sometimes as part of a longer event or seminar, like a yoga conference. Janine Liberty, one of our research associates, attended such an evening in April 2010, along with about a thousand others. When Chopra asked for a show of hands from those who had heard him speak before, she estimated that at least 10 percent had.

Chopra also maintains his current presence on the web. As of late 2012, Chopra had nearly 1.2 million followers on Twitter and his official Facebook page had over four hundred thousand "likes."

This kind of rapid and dense cadence, while creating a good deal of respiration, also has its downsides. The most obvious one is the danger that the material may wear thin. It seems impossible for Chopra to have accumulated enough material himself, with care, to fill up all those books, which means the content no longer connects so directly to his original fascination and personal narrative, and begins to feel less genuine. Chopra now seems more like a "personality" of the ideaplex than an idea entrepreneur.

Sustainable

Even when they do create mutually animating platforms, formal organizations, and multifaceted enterprises—no matter how large and sprawling they may be—the idea entrepreneur, the individual, typically remains at the center of it all. Although Blake Mycoskie may want to separate himself from the story, Eckhart Tolle speaks to his audiences through his partner and on television, and Al Gore enlists surrogates, the idea, the person, the organization remain more or less as one. There could be no dog-centered TV show without Cesar Millan, no one-day course without Edward Tufte, no day in Paris without Mireille Guiliano, no lecture without Emerson, no evening with Chopra without Deepak himself.

Idea entrepreneurs rarely think about creating an enterprise that is built to operate without them and last beyond them. They are not typically the professional corporate soldiers, after all, who have the skills or experience of organization building. They are not naturally inclined to the work of regularizing processes, creating leadership teams, allocating resources, managing succession, selling the company or taking it public, and handing over the reins one day (however reluctantly). Because idea entrepreneurs have intertwined the idea so tightly with their own personal narratives, and because the organizations have been created expressly to leverage their personal time and energy, it is almost impossible to disentangle the elements. Whatever the actual name of their foundation or institute or center may be, it is the idea entrepreneur's name that really matters.

Having expressed the idea, built a life around it, and taken it public is enough for many an idea entrepreneur. Besides, their fascination may not be fundamental enough, or their idea may not touch an issue that is universal enough, to really warrant an effort that spans more than a single working lifespan, or necessitate an effort continuing across many generations. Will American obesity be a central issue twenty years hence? Probably. Will Chinese parenting cause such a ruckus in the future? Maybe. Will lousy visual displays of information still be tormenting us a generation on? Highly likely. But will the specific ideas, narratives, and practices of Guiliano, Chua, and Tufte still be relevant? Very possibly; very possibly not.

However, a few idea entrepreneurs do think in the very long term. We don't have much to go on in this regard, because most members of what I think of as the first generation of idea entrepreneurs are still on the scene and hard at work, but a few of them seem to be thinking about what happens after they're gone.

Stephen Covey, who died in 2012, is one idea entrepreneur who built an enterprise that seems designed to outlive him. Franklin-

Covey, which Dr. Covey cofounded, is a for-profit organization that offers various products and services, including training and speaking, and Covey has a very large body of mutually animating expressions—books and "book tools," as they are described on the Covey website—that can continue to deliver the idea.[38] But what about new expressions? Conversation? Current presence? Further accumulation? Additions to the personal narrative?

There are indications that the Covey enterprise has not quite determined how to continue without its idea entrepreneur at the center. Dr. Covey died in mid-July of 2012 and, as of early September, the website—although the home page acknowledged his death—was still speaking of him in the present tense: "Would you like Dr. Covey to speak at your event or organization? Click here for more information."[39]

AFTER ME

Perhaps the most intriguing example of an idea entrepreneur who, after decades of being the cynosure of his effort, is deliberately removing himself from the center of attention comes from India. I speak of the Sulabh International Social Organisation, based in Delhi, and its founder and leader, Dr. Bindeshwar Pathak. Now approaching the age of seventy, Pathak takes the very long-term view, largely because his issue is such a huge and intractable one. His idea goes to the very heart of Indian society; it involves the disruption of a deeply entrenched status quo and requires the infecting of millions of minds. Although he has developed a great deal of influence in his work, he can see that there is a long way to go.

Pathak's fascination, and his lifework, center around one of the most perplexing issues of Indian life: sanitation. Pathak's sacred expression is not a book, or a map, or a video, or a blog—although he has created all of those. It is, rather, a technology, a tangible, a form of merchandise (although Pathak's enterprise is a not-for-profit): a toilet. A water closet that requires very little water. A commode that does not demand a fancy bathroom surrounding it. And an essential part of Pathak's mutually animating platform of expressions is the practice that goes along with the toilet, which is, of course, the using of it.

This issue of sanitation might seem as fundamental as an issue can get, but it connects with an even deeper and more universal social issue in India: class inequality, the caste system, and, in particular, the plight of the untouchables.

Starting in 1968, Dr. Pathak has successfully taken his idea public. He has done so through books, which include *Road to Freedom: A Sociological Study on the Abolition of Scavenging in India*. Although they could not be described as best-sellers, they have been influential and reached an immediate audience in such a way that Pathak is a respected voice in the conversation. He has worked the global ideaplex such that he and his ideas have been the subject of articles and stories worldwide. Although Americans likely have not heard of him, he has been recognized by international leaders, from the former president of India, Shri R. Venkataraman, to Pope John Paul II, who gave him an audience when he was awarded the St. Francis Prize for the Environment.

And, along the way, Pathak has built an enterprise. Note that its name is Sulabh International—*sulabh* means "simple," although it has by now become an eponym for toilet, as Kleenex is an eponym for tissue—rather than the Pathak Foundation or the like.

In the summer of 2011, Anna and I—again accompanied by our associate, researcher and journalist Mridu Khullar Relph—met with Dr. Pathak in Delhi and were treated to a complete and memorable tour of the Sulabh facilities. The visit began with a welcome by the elegant Dr. Pathak and his associate Anita Jha, a small squad of photographers and videographers hovering nearby. We then took part in the morning prayer, which was attended by a group that included students from the Vocational Training Center that is part of the Sulabh facility, as well as ten or twelve women who—thanks to Sulabh's efforts—had been lifted from their former lives as scavengers, India's lowest societal group. We then toured the Sulabh Public School, the Sulabh Vocational, and strolled through the Sulabh International Museum of Toilets. We were also shown a potential future energy source for India: hardened balls of dried excreta, now completely pathogen-free. "Smell them!" our guide commanded. We did. Totally odorless.

At last we came to the heart of the matter: several different models of the Sulabh toilet, arrayed around another outdoor space. These ranged from a modest version constructed of inexpensive materials to a top-of-the-line model, constructed of cement and finished with tile.

We ended our visit with an extended interview with Dr. Pathak, followed by lunch—eaten in complete silence—in a cool, dimly lit room. During our time with him, Dr. Pathak made it clear that Sulabh International was no longer about him. Yes, he continued to be the ambassador, the spokesperson, the man whose picture adorned the walls of the dining room, but the idea had gained enough respiration and had been so completely expressed in so many ways, and detailed in such specific and replicable practices, that it no longer required his direct engagement. Indeed, it was imperative for him to step away, to bring others forward, and disconnect his own narrative—which he proceeded to relate to us—from that of the idea.

Fundamental Fascination

The roots of Pathak's fascination go back to his early life, as they so often do with the idea entrepreneur. He was born in 1943 in the village of Rampur Baghel in the Vaishali district of Bihar, some five hundred kilometers to the northwest of Kolkata. His family was Brahmin, the highest of India's castes.

Pathak's grandfather had amassed considerable wealth from the practice of astrology. The family lived in a large home with gardens and owned several pieces of land in the area, totaling some two hundred acres. But, even as grand as the Pathak house was, with its own well to draw water, it had, as was typical, no indoor toilets.

"My mother, my grandmother, my aunties, they all used to wake up in the morning at four o'clock and go outside" to do their business, Pathak told Khullar Relph. During his childhood, Pathak studied at four different schools, none of which had a toilet.

The Pathak house employed many workers from the area. One woman who came to the house particularly intrigued young Bindeshwar, then about ten years old. A curious thing happened after the woman left: his grandmother would sprinkle water where the woman had stepped. *Why does she do that*, he wondered. *Because the woman is untouchable*, he was told. The water purified the places where she had walked.

Untouchable? What would happen if he did touch her, Bindeshwar wondered. Would it cause something strange to happen? One day, as he passed the woman in a hallway, his fascination got the better of him. He touched her. Nothing strange happened. He did it again another day. Still nothing.

Then some time later, just as he touched the woman, his grandmother witnessed the transgression. She raised a "hue and cry," as Pathak called it. *Bindeshwar has touched an untouchable! How can he live in the house now?* His mother tried to calm things down, to no avail. He would have to be purified.

Grandmother forced the boy to follow the ancient custom: to swallow cow dung, drink cow urine, and drink a draft of water from the Ganges. The kind of iconic moment one does not easily, if ever, forget.

Social Connection

With that single touch, Pathak had connected in a way that few others of his class had with something essential about his nation and its culture: poor sanitation. It remains a huge problem for India, even today. As Khullar Relph wrote in *Time* magazine in 2009, "Some 110 million households remain without access to a toilet and 75 percent of the country's surface water is contaminated by human and agricultural waste. More than half a million children die each year from preventable water- and sanitation-related diseases such as diarrhea, cholera and hepatitis."[40]

What's more, millions of Indian households rely on bucket toilets, which are exactly what they sound like they are: buckets with no connection to a central sewer system, no flushing mechanism, and no covering. The practice of "scavenging" is the manual transfer of human waste, known as "night soil," from the buckets into vessels that the scavengers carry on their heads to disposal sites. Scavengers have been branded for centuries as untouchables and have traditionally been banned from regular interaction with society and from seeking or doing any other kind of work. "The person born untouchable will die as untouchable," Pathak told us. It is like being in a "social prison" where there is "no chance of escape."

It is an ancient practice, going back many millennia, and has long been recognized as a problem. Pathak told us that Gandhi first called for Indian independence from Great Britain and then said, "I want to see India clean." Gandhi tried to model better sanitation habits and pushed for legislation that would enforce them, but he did not influence much change nor did he accomplish the eradication of the scavenger class. V. S. Naipaul, the writer who was born in Trinidad to parents of Indian heritage, described the problem vividly in his book *An Area of Darkness*, published in 1964. Gandhi, he says, saw that "sanitation was linked to caste," and that caste had created a "hopelessly divided country," which led to national weakness that had enabled rule by a foreign country. "This is what Gandhi saw," Naipaul writes, "and no one purely of India could have seen it."[41]

But Pathak, purely of India, did see that, although it took him some time to do so, and the revelation happened almost accidentally.

Pathak's family lost all its wealth when he was still a boy, so he could no longer look forward to a privileged life as a landowner. He earned an undergraduate degree at the University of Patna, and after graduating in 1964 at the age of twenty-one, he returned to his village and took a job as a teacher. He soon married and, in need of more income, quit teaching and went to work with his father, but this did not suit him.

He enrolled in a master's degree program at Patna, focusing on sociology, and there became involved with the Bihar Gandhi Centenary Celebrations Committee. (Pathak eventually went on to earn a PhD in sociology as well as a master's degree in English and a DLitt.) The job of the Celebrations Committee was to make plans for the hundredth anniversary of Gandhi's birth, which would come around in 1969. The general secretary of the committee determined that, as a tribute to Gandhi, Pathak should try to realize the Mahatma's goal: to find alternatives to the age-old system of scavenging and, as a result, restore the human rights and dignity of the untouchables.

"How can I do this?" Pathak asked the general secretary. "I am a Brahmin. I am not an engineer. What can I do?" If Gandhi had been unable to put a dent in the problem, how could he?

The secretary gazed at him. "I see light in you," he said to Pathak. "I do not know whether you're a Brahmin, or an engineer, but you can do this."

Iconic Moments

Pathak at last agreed. He took on the task as a sociologist would: he went to live in a colony of untouchables and scavengers in Champaran, an area of Bihar, and one of the colonies that Gandhi, too, had visited in 1917.[42]

This went against everything he had been taught and experienced. "Always we were told, 'Don't, don't, don't. Don't touch. Don't take water from their hands. Don't eat food from their hands,'" Pathak told us. "But, I thought, unless I go there and live there, I cannot know them."

On the first day in Champaran, he visited with some of the scavengers in their dwellings, and managed to talk with them a little. On the second day he entered a toilet, but found it so disgusting he could barely bring himself to go inside. He took a broom and a can of water and began to clean it himself. The villagers watched. In time, they began to clean the toilets themselves, too.

Gradually, Pathak was accepted by the untouchables. He talked with them, took meals with them, and eventually felt that he could try to influence their habits directly. One day he heard an altercation of some kind. A young woman of the colony "was being forced to go and clean bucket toilets by her in-laws and husband himself," Pathak said. "She was crying bitterly." He tried to intervene, but the young woman's mother-in-law spoke up. As a member of an untouchable family there was no other work the girl could do. "If she sells vegetables, who will buy from her hands?" the mother-in-law asked. Pathak had no answer. The girl went to clean the toilets.

There came another experience, which became Pathak's catalyst toward idea entrepreneurship, to breaking out. One day he watched as a young boy, wearing a bright red shirt, was charged by a bull. People rushed forward to rescue him until someone screamed that the boy lived in the scavenger colony. Everybody stopped short. At last, Pathak and a few others pulled the boy away from the bull and rushed him to the hospital. It was too late. "It was there in the hospital itself that I took a vow to fulfill the dreams of Mahatma Gandhi," Pathak said.

A Solution in Three Sentences

But how? Pathak knew that the speaking and writing of an unknown member of the Brahmin caste would surely have no effect on his countrymen. If Gandhi's railing against the caste system, the suffering of the scavengers, and the collecting of night soil had provoked no change, what could he hope for?

He read everything he could get his hands on about sanitation in developing societies. He happened upon a passage in a book published by the World Health Organization called, with exquisite specificity, *Excreta Disposal for Rural Areas and Small Communities*. In one passage, the author described a certain kind of toilet, a sanitary pit, that seemed like it would fill the bill in India. "Those three or four sentences," Pathak said, "were the genesis of the whole Sulabh movement."

Pathak adapted the system, the Sulabh Sauchalaya, so it would be practicable for installation and use in India. The toilet, comprising two pits used alternately, requires only a small amount of water for flushing, so it does not need to be hooked into a water or sewer infrastructure, both of which are hard to come by in India, especially in rural areas. It can be made very cheaply, is easy to install and simple to maintain, and does not need to be emptied. Over a period of two years, the collected waste is transformed into toxin-free manure that can eventually be removed safely and used as fertilizer for farming. The pit size is designed in such a way that it can be cleaned in a cycle of a minimum of four years (with each pit being used alternately for a period of two years each) and, in total, the toilet can serve for up to forty years—with each pit in use for twenty years.

Pathak wrote about the toilet, the system, the design, the practices, and how it might be installed throughout the region. He decided to start promoting his idea in his home area of Patna, but he soon learned that he could not influence people's thinking or their behavior simply by introducing them to this new and different technology—the strange object associated with an unaccustomed practice.

He needed some help and support and thought it might come from the local officials. Wrong. He sought permission to install some demonstration toilets in the area. The local official was having none of it. "He said, humbug," Pathak told us. "Nothing doing. I will not allow a single toilet of Sulabh to be built in the Patna town!"

Pathak did not give up. He decided to apply for a small government grant to fund the creation of his organization. He went to visit the appropriate official and found him to be more accommodating. He had read Pathak's work and was impressed. "Your program is going to create a great impact in this country," he said.

The official had a piece of advice regarding the organization and how it should best fund itself. "Do not take this grant," he told Pathak. A government grant would only restrict the organization, he counseled, and tie it up with regulations and inspections and all sorts of folderol. Apply instead for funds to pay for the implementation of specific projects, he advised, which would provide a small fee for each toilet installation. By taking fees for projects, rather than receiving grants to run an organization, Pathak was free to operate as he wished. Any extra money from the installations could be used to support the Sulabh organization. It was a partnership of government and nongovernment organizations that set the pattern Pathak still follows today.

Another government official also took it upon himself to visit the local authorities to clear the way for Pathak. "Let him put up 200 toilets in the Patna town," the government official said. "If it becomes successful, it will change the course of history of sanitation in India. If not successful, we will stop it. But I cannot agree with you that new ideas should not be tried.'" And that was the beginning, Pathak told us, "the ray of hope."

Endorsers

To be paid for the delivery of services required that a service be delivered, which meant actually installing a toilet in someone's home. No one, Pathak found, was interested. He went from house to house describing his Sulabh toilet.

Pathak quickly discovered that even that approach was going to be tricky. In the late 1960s, nobody wanted to talk about toilets. (It is still not a popular topic.) "I used to go and meet people and they would warn me that you can talk about everything, but not about toilets," he said. Even if he could get a conversation started it was usually with the men, not the women, who were often the ones who most wanted the privacy of a toilet. "The entire family used to come and sit with me, but not the women." But all was not lost. The women would station themselves outside the room and behind a door, peering in, he said, so they could hear the conversation although they rarely entered into it.

After several months of talking, having convinced not a single person to install one of his Sulabh toilets, Pathak needed a fresh approach. He was in need of his version of Jada Pinkett Smith, who championed Millan, or Guiliano's friend who had urged her to write the book, or Kevin Salwen's friend who got them on the *Today* show. Pathak found his entry to the (admittedly rudimentary) ideaplex through the actions of another local official, Suresh Prasad Singh, who, wonder of wonders, asked Pathak to install a toilet in his house.

Once it was in place, his neighbors and other people in the village started coming to see what all the fuss was about. They saw the object. They heard about the practice of using an enclosed toilet that did not involve a bucket that needed to be emptied each morning. They connected the object with the talk they had heard from this fellow Pathak. One by one, they started installing the Sulabh toilets in their homes, too.

Pathak's work, however, did not always gain him favor with those close to him. His in-laws did not approve. The Brahmin community shunned him. "It was becoming beyond my endurance," he said. He virtually became an untouchable himself. "No one would be allowed to sit with me," he told Khullar Relph. "They'd say, no no, you're the scavengers' leader. Sit at a little distance." Friends from college, who had once held high regard for Pathak's intelligence, would say, *The genius has been spoiled.* Only his mother and his wife refused to speak a word against him.

Institution

Jumping ahead several decades, we find that Pathak's idea, which he had adapted from Gandhi and others before him, has influenced thinking and affected behavior throughout India.

Today, Sulabh International is a multifaceted enterprise. Most important, Sulabh gives the toilet design away for free and holds no patents on it (which might be hard to get, anyway, given how uncomplicated it is). This produces no revenue but generates substantial and continuing respiration. Sulabh derives revenue from three main activities. First, they do the work of converting bucket toilets in private homes into Sulabh sanitary pits—which frees the local scavengers from their social prisons—and also install new ones, for which they receive a small supervision fee. Second, Sulabh builds public toilets, also for a supervision fee, which is calculated as 15 to 20 percent of the project cost, and also maintains about 8,000 toilets in India. Third, Sulabh cleans public buildings, such as hospitals and government offices, including the house of the president of India, which also generates revenue.

The money is reinvested in maintaining the organizational infrastructure and existing work, conducting research and development (Sulabh is perfecting the use of human waste for the production of electricity) for the creation of new expressions—publications, conferences, seminars—and, finally, in improving the welfare of the poor and underserved. Sulabh and the World Toilet Organization jointly organized their own version of the TED talk, focused solely on sanitation. The World Toilet Summit convened in 2007 and attracted representatives from countries around the world.[43]

Dr. Pathak has certainly had an influence on the minds and behaviors of the people of India, and his organization is careful to evaluate its efforts through metrics. Sulabh reckons that, thanks to their efforts, more than a million of its toilets have been constructed and an equal number of scavengers have been liberated and rehabilitated; some 640 towns have been made scavenger-free; and an estimated 10 million plus people use Sulabh or Sulabh-design toilets every day.[44] In 2004, 27 percent of the inhabitants of rural India had access to a toilet. By 2009, some 59 percent did.[45] Over fifty thousand people volunteer with the Sulabh organization.[46]

Thanks to all this activity, Sulabh has achieved the status of a respected, sustainable enterprise that has become a valued part of the country's social fabric—and which is no longer completely synonymous with Dr. Pathak and his narrative, as important as both still are.

As proof of this status, Khullar Relph told us about another important and relevant metric that has arisen largely thanks to Sulabh's efforts—although it is a little more difficult to quantify than the number of toilets installed. It is this: young Indian women— who once might have been like those who lingered behind the door as the conversation turned to sanitation—have added a new criterion to their list when evaluating a potential husband. He must have a toilet installed in the house.

It took forty-plus years and a lifetime of effort to accomplish it, but now the Sulabh idea has become part of a society's train of thought, a key element of what I call the *thinking journey*.

6

THE THINKING
JOURNEY

As with the development of all the ideas discussed in this book, I too experienced revelatory moments in the development of my own idea. One of them came, unexpectedly, during my conversation with Cesar Millan. I asked him if he had any models, people whom he admired and respected and in whose footsteps he hoped to follow.

"Everybody that goes against society," he said. But, he quickly added, "not like a rebel, not like a Jesse James." He was thinking, he explained, of people like Martin Luther King and John F. Kennedy, and particularly of the famous line from JFK's inaugural speech: "Ask not what your country can do for you—ask what you can do for your country."

That's because Millan, in addition to his work on individual dog-human relationships, has a meta concern: our national disposition toward the dog population and how we manage it. Millan wants more people to adopt dogs and spay and neuter them so that the canine birthrate will decrease and the number of dogs who are "put down" each year—which he estimates to be around four and a half million, of both unwanted puppies and mature dogs—will also decrease.[1]

Then came the revelation.

"Gandhi has a quote," Millan said. "'The greatness of a nation and the morality of its values can be measured by the way we treat our animals.' I take that in consideration a lot and I want to plant that quote in everybody's mind." (Gandhi said it a little differently than Cesar remembered, but the sense is the same.)

The comment struck me in two ways. First, I had not expected Millan to cite Gandhi as a model. But he was not the only one to do so. Of course, there was Dr. Bindeshwar Pathak, who was directly inspired by Gandhi and operated within his country and even focused on the same issue. But other idea entrepreneurs and people we interviewed also mentioned Gandhi, or people who followed the Gandhi model, as an inspiration—even if they didn't have a very accurate picture of what Gandhi did or exactly how he pursued his goals. So Millan's comment helped me understand that all idea entrepreneurs tend to think of themselves—more or less like Gandhi—as crusaders in a cause, leaders of movements, change makers and rebels against a status quo.

The other striking aspect of Millan's comment was the part about wanting to "plant" his idea in the minds of others. This, it seemed to me, describes the activity of the idea entrepreneur as brilliantly and simply as does Tolstoy's description of infecting the minds of others. To idea entrepreneurs, the idea is a seed. Their method is to plant it so that it takes root in individual minds. Their goal is that the planted idea will influence how those individuals think and behave and, when many individuals are affected, that a larger cultural change will take place.

TRUTH FIRMNESS

There was more in Millan's comment. The more I thought about his particular method of working with dogs—and of the description of how an idea entrepreneur plants an idea in others' minds—a deeper, subtler, and ultimately more important connection between Millan and Gandhi and all idea entrepreneurs emerged. A central tenet of Millan's method for working with dogs is the practice of what he calls "calm assertiveness."

He might just as well have called it *satyagraha*.

Satyagraha is a Sanskrit word (a neologism, actually, that one of Gandhi's followers, Maganlal Gandhi, coined and Gandhi adopted[2]) that means "truth firmness" or "truth force." It underlies the practice of nonviolent resistance that Gandhi used so often in his life and that others, including King, followed as well. Gandhi, in his autobiography, talks again and again about the method of speaking calmly, powerfully, even assertively, but always with the goal of helping the other understand an idea—of planting it—so it could be considered and, hopefully, acted upon.

So I came to think of Cesar Millan and Mohandas Gandhi, as unlikely as it might have seemed at first, as two figures who were both involved in what I ended up calling a *thinking journey*—the development of an idea over time, through the participation of many people.

The thinking journey of the *satyagraha*/calm assertiveness approach is quite easy to trace and brings in another player who figures in this book, Henry David Thoreau, and his concept of living deliberately/civil disobedience. We know, for example, that Tolstoy read Thoreau, because he cited Thoreau's works in his book *The Circle of Reading,* a collection of quotes and citations from writers around the world.[3] We also know that Gandhi read both Tolstoy and Thoreau. He translated portions of Thoreau's *Civil Disobedience* and published them in his chronicle *Indian Opinion. Indian Opinion* even ran an essay-writing competition in 1907, asking readers to consider "The Ethics of Passive Resistance" as expressed in Thoreau's *On the Duty of Civil Disobedience,* Tolstoy's *The Kingdom of God Is Within You,* and the *Apology of Socrates.*[4] (Quite an assignment.)

We can also trace the journey further back in time, and see that it is a universal idea that has been developed over a period of centuries, even millennia. In an introduction to *Walden,* author and naturalist Bill McKibben writes that Thoreau "is the American incarnation in a line of crackpots and gurus from Buddha on."[5] We know that Thoreau was familiar with the *Vedas,* the early Indian sacred text that he mentions in *Walden,* and no doubt fed his ideas.[6] The idea stream flows from Thoreau to Gandhi, although it strays northward a bit to infect Tolstoy and then flows forward to the names I have already mentioned.

Gandhi considered both Thoreau's and Tolstoy's ideas as he developed *satyagraha* which underlies his practice of nonviolent resistance, which is akin to Thoreau's civil disobedience, and which later inspired Martin Luther King and others around the world, including Cesar Millan and others in this book.

So the Russian genius (also possibly a crackpot), the father of the Indian nation, and the leader of the American civil rights movement give some credit to Thoreau for their thinking and their actions, and he, in turn, looks back to earlier influencers. Over the centuries and in different countries and in a wide variety of disciplines and activities, millions of other people have considered the idea, and put it into practice in their own way. The idea plants itself deep in the mind of a culture.

Indeed, all of the idea entrepreneurs I have considered in this book embrace, to a greater or lesser degree, the practice of truth firmness. They are not rebels, like Jesse James. They do not generally revile those who disagree with them. (Millan may joke about Harvard-trained dog owners, but in a kind-spirited way.) They seek to influence the thinking of others, not repress or dismiss it. They want change, not power.

No One Thinks Alone

The development of truth firmness is one example of a thinking journey. All of the elements we have talked about—the personal narrative, the expressions, the response of the ideaplex and multiple audiences, respiration in its many forms, the audiences, surfacing of cultural tensions, the rebuttal and backlash, the twists and turns in the narrative—contribute to any thinking journey.

No one creates a really powerful and lasting idea alone and no one takes a thinking journey alone. So, as we try to deal with the idea glut we face today, it can be helpful to consider the thinking journey it might be a part of. Where did the idea spring from? What fascinates us about it? What were the revelation points along the way? What other ideas had to be abandoned or displaced to make room for the new one? What material has accumulated around it? Who else has been involved in its development? What were people's objections to it? What debate swirled around it? How did it fare in the ideaplex? What connection or disconnection did it have with the zeitgeist? How does it connect to *other* ideas, narratives, and thinking journeys—current, long past, and to come in the future?

We cannot all be Thoreaus or Tolstoys or Gandhis or Kings, nor do we want to be. But it's important for the idea entrepreneur to keep in mind that, while the act of breaking out brings a great deal of personal attention, the effort must be understood as in service of the idea, not the person, and, ultimately, seen as a means of helping other people, addressing important issues of benefit to many, and improving society as a whole.

WORK VIRTUE

Not all idea entrepreneurs, however, think of themselves as contributors to the truth-firmness thinking journey, especially those who have a strong emphasis on the entrepreneur part of idea entrepreneurship.

When I asked Blake Mycoskie, for example, if he had a hero, someone he admired and who had served as a model for his one-for-one enterprise, TOMS Shoes, he mentioned neither Mohandas Gandhi nor Henry David Thoreau. He did come up with three very interesting models, however.

Number one, Ted Turner, the founder of CNN and philanthropist donor of $1 billion to the United Nations. (Plus, more recently, the mastermind behind Ted's Montana Grill, which features National Bison Association–certified bison meatloaf.) Second was Muhammad Yunus, the Bangladeshi Nobel Prize winner and founder of the Grameen Bank, one of the pioneers of microcredit. The third was Mary Kay Ash, founder of Mary Kay Cosmetics, the direct sales (a.k.a. pyramid or home party plan) company that offers a variety of products primarily sold by and to women around the world, and winner, among many other honors, of the Horatio Alger Award for 1978.

A very interesting mixture: a classic business entrepreneur turned philanthropist, a social activist promoting new approaches to business, and a businessperson whose model is based on both profit and personal improvement.

Which brings us to the hidden forebear of a thinking journey that runs parallel to the "truth firmness" path, an idea that can be found planted in the minds of most idea entrepreneurs—whether or not they acknowledge or admit it. It is a concept that is even more fundamental, and perhaps more widely held, than Thoreau's notion of living deliberately: that through hard work and personal effort anyone can improve himself and his circumstances.

An Earlier Idea Entrepreneur

For the origins of this idea, we must lurch back a century or so prior to Thoreau's time, to Ben Franklin. I think of Franklin as our earliest idea entrepreneur because he was not only a master of the ideaplex but also one of its inventors, primarily through the creation of his publication *Poor Richard's Almanack*. It was a best-seller for its day, selling ten thousand copies a year for all twenty-eight years of its publication, starting in 1732.[7] In addition to the *Almanack,* Franklin published a newspaper and a magazine, and, in a clever bit of platform building, ran printing operations and franchised them through partners in other colonies.

Franklin also founded an early version of the TED talk called Junto. The Junto particularly loved to crash together ideas and viewpoints across boundaries, as does TED.

Franklin's idea—that there is virtue in hard work—hardly sounds rebellious or heterodox now, as it has become so embedded in our cultural mind, but it was so during Franklin's time. The prevailing idea then was that virtue resided in godliness, hard work was reserved for the laboring class and hardly represented virtue, and upward mobility was frowned upon. Franklin was fascinated by hard work and modeled it in his own life, which has become one of our most durable personal up-by-the-bootstraps narratives.

It's important to add that Gandhi embraced this thinking journey as well. Like Franklin, he was an exceptionally hard worker, and he was well known for his facility with expression and his ability to take his ideas public through a variety of channels. In an article in *Economic & Political Weekly,* Leonard A. Gordon refers to Gandhi as a "media expert who had early on discovered that spreading his point of view to concerned audiences was a vital part of successful political activity."[8] How else could Gandhi have landed on the cover of *Time* magazine as its Man of the Year for 1930, having never visited the United States and being virtually unknown here?

Both Franklin and Gandhi understood quite well what they were doing and both were mindful of how they managed the ideaplex of the day. According to his *Autobiography,* Franklin experienced just the kind of revelations and turning points we have seen with others, developments that contributed to the evolution of his idea.

As wildly popular as Franklin was during his lifetime (1706–1790), he has had his ups and downs since his death. As the thinkers of the Enlightenment (Diderot, Voltaire, Montesquieu) who had influenced Franklin and Thomas Jefferson and others in America gave way to the Romantics, Franklin fell out of favor. Poet John Keats (1795–1821) went so far as to say that Ben Franklin was a "not sublime man," and the dissing kept coming.[9] A century later, author D. H. Lawrence (1885–1930), described our hero as "[m]iddle-sized, sturdy, snuff-coloured Doctor Franklin, one of the soundest citizens that ever trod or 'used venery.'" Lawrence concluded, simply, "I do not like him."[10] For Lawrence, Franklin's idea of virtue was a "barbed wire fence" that traps people inside, stifling their creative instinct, their passion, their poetry.[11]

Ben Meets Ragged Dick

The Franklin idea got a boost in this country from a writer and observer of lesser literary stature than Keats or Lawrence, but of great popular renown. I refer to Horatio Alger Jr., who wrote a series of novels primarily for the entertainment and moral education of young American boys. We largely have Alger to thank for the rags-to-riches narrative that still inspires, even if Alger's books—the two most famous of which are *Ragged Dick* (1868) and its sequel, *Fame and Fortune* (1868)—are pretty much forgotten. In them we follow the narrative of young Richard Hunter, a.k.a. Ragged Dick, as he rises from bootblack to junior partner in a prosperous firm in nineteenth-century New York.

Although few people read Alger today except in the cause of cultural research, we still hear the phrase a "Horatio Alger–like story," even if the person making the reference may not know anything about Horatio Alger or his work. Of course, it is not necessary to read the books to know what they're about, which is essentially the fictionalized version of Franklin's message: that with ambition and hard work, anyone can achieve success in America. Pluck, good nature, honesty, courage, loyalty, generosity, perseverance, study, moral rectitude, the ability to attract mentors and sponsors, and a bit of luck will pay off—even if one lacks formal education and social status.

Some of the elements of Dick's narrative line up quite wonderfully with Franklin's, and resonate with some of the stories of the idea entrepreneur today—there are, for example, always fascinations, iconic scenes, and moments of revelation. For both Franklin and Dick, these include heroic moments that involve acts of physical bravery—for example, both Franklin and Ragged Dick, expert swimmers, save a stranger from drowning. Ragged Dick Hunter, on an outing with a friend on a New York ferry, observes a little boy fall overboard and, without hesitation, leaps into the river to save him. His good deed is well rewarded by the boy's father, James Rockwell, who eventually invites him to join his firm at the outrageous wage of $10 per week. Dick eventually becomes his business partner.

Revelations create turning points in the narrative for Franklin as well. In November of 1724, when Franklin was just eighteen but already an experienced printer and publisher, he connected with Sir William Keith, who became a mentor/patron of sorts. Sir William dispatched Franklin to London to better learn his trade, along with guarantees of financial support and promises to set Franklin up in a business in Philadelphia upon his return. Turns out that Sir William, although well meaning, did not have two shillings to rub together, at least not on Franklin's behalf. Franklin discovered this only after arriving in London, finding himself without funds, credit, a job, or reason to be there. Franklin then showed himself as Franklin. He made the most of a bad situation, found work at big London printing houses, worked hard, and learned a good deal. In July of 1726, he returned to Philadelphia with a determination to become a reliable person, and no doubt also with a distrust of the aristocracy that had let him down, expressed in his "Plan for Future Conduct." Incident led to revelation: *he would have to rely on himself.* Franklin went on to become a self-made man, financially successful, and internationally famous. Sir William, on the other hand, drove deep into debt, ended up in financial despair, and died in the Old Bailey, the prison in West London.

Just as we can follow Thoreau's thinking journey back to Buddha and forward to Cesar Millan, so can we do the same with Franklin's idea—although it has fewer obvious antecedents and is much more an indigenous American idea, perhaps *the* American idea.

But we can certainly carry his idea forward through Alger and Thomas Edison to Tom Peters, Stephen Covey, Steve Jobs, and Blake Mycoskie.

MYTHOLOGIZING

When idea entrepreneurs combine these two elements—the idea of truth firmness and the idea of hard work as a means of creating virtue—their narratives may sometimes approach the status of myths, along the lines of Gandhi and Franklin.

Of course, the ideaplex is only too willing to help the idea entrepreneur in this effort. The media are relentless mythologizers, seeking to compress long narratives into easily digestible nuggets. And our apprehension methods—the very way our brains work—also contribute; even if we really do read the book or watch the video or attend the talk, what tends to remain in the mind are the emblems and iconic moments, the aphorisms and practices, the little bits and pieces that somehow connect for us.

And, because we respond so strongly to stories, especially personal stories that involve hardship and struggle and the overcoming of obstacles, it's no wonder that the events of the idea entrepreneur's life can take on such significance.

Pitfalls

Mythologizing is to be diligently avoided, however, because when the idea entrepreneur wanders into such terrain, the path is almost sure to lead toward traps and pitfalls—which can cause serious damage to the idea, especially if the idea entrepreneur is still on the scene and publicly stumbles.

This happened with Franklin and also with Horatio Alger Jr., who—I am sorry to have to reveal, for those who care but do not know—was suspected of child molestation, which cast a shadow over his career and his long-term influence. Greg Mortenson is a more recent and obvious example of an idea entrepreneur whose myth doesn't quite track with his reality.

Mortenson is the hugely successful advocate of the idea that the education of young girls in troubled countries, like Afghanistan, can lead to the end of terrorism and the establishment of long-term peace. His sacred expression is the book *Three Cups of Tea: One Man's Mission to Promote Peace . . . One School at a Time* (Penguin, 2007), which has sold in the neighborhood of three and half million copies, and the follow-up *Stones into Schools: Promoting Peace with Books, Not Bombs, in Afghanistan and Pakistan* (Viking, 2009), which sold nearly a half million copies in the United States alone.

Just as the title says, the book tells the story of Mortenson's individual mission, which started with a personal quest that went awry—an attempt to honor his dead sister by scaling K2. His failure to accomplish that goal led to a revelation in an Afghan village and, eventually, to the founding of schools; the creation of an institution, the Central Asia Institute; the development of school curricula; and enough political influence that Mortenson has been consulted by the U.S. State Department in an attempt to tap his extensive knowledge of the region. Mortenson gives as many as 160 public appearances each year and was nominated for the Nobel Peace Prize, although he did not win.[12]

Ah, but did Mortenson really do all of that? Did all those things actually happen? Writer Jon Krakauer, Mortenson's former friend and ex-supporter, has his doubts. In 2011, Krakauer published a monograph called *Three Cups of Deceit: How Greg Mortenson, Humanitarian Hero, Lost His Way,* in which he calls into question some of the iconic events and revelations that have become central to Mortenson's narrative. Did he really wander into that Afghan village at all, Krakauer asks. How many schools has Mortenson really founded? Is his idea really sound? Krakauer writes, "[T]he multitudes who have bought *Three Cups* haven't merely read it; they've embraced it with singular passion."[13] That is partly due, he continues, to "its forceful, uncomplicated theme—terrorism can be eradicated by educating children in impoverished societies—and its portrayal of Mortenson as a humble, Gandhi-like figure who has repeatedly risked life and limb to advance his humanitarian agenda."[14] Krakauer's critique has not done nearly as well as Mortenson's, which suggests that people are more captivated by personal missions to promote peace than campaigns to defame the promoters—and that it is very tough to dispel a myth once it has become established, has connected with the zeitgeist, and has served to articulate the thoughts of a large number of people.

The Krakauer kerfuffle was not the end of Mortenson's troubles. Money, which can be a chronic source of difficulty for the idea entrepreneur, further complicated matters. In 2011, Mortenson was investigated by the attorney general of the state of Montana, where his Central Asia Institute (CAI) is headquartered, for allegations of misuse of the organization's funds. He was suspected of using charitable donations for charter flights and family travel as well as personal items. The institute, it was charged, also had purchased nearly $4 million worth of Mortenson's books from online retailers to be distributed free, but Mortenson collected the royalties on the sales. The investigation also looked into his speaking fees—which were in the range of $25,000–$35,000 per talk—most of which he pocketed, rather than deposited into CAI's coffers. Mortenson was forced to resign as executive director of the institute he founded, remove himself as a voting member from the board, and pay back around $1 million. Even despite his supposed transgressions, CAI was in good financial health, with over $20 million in reserves in April of 2012.[15] (In a cruel twist, the coauthor of *Three Cups of Tea*, David Oliver Relin, committed suicide in late 2012. According to an obituary in the *New York Times*, Relin had been depressed and "suffered emotionally and financially as basic facts in the book were called into question."[16])

Mortenson's reputation took a hit in all this but, as with every debate and instance of backlash, it brought out his supporters in an antibacklash backlash, many of whom argued that the details did not matter. It made no difference if Mortenson did not have his revelation in exactly the way he relates in his book. Nor did it make any difference that he may not have built as many schools as he claims. Or that he was not a good manager of money. *No one ever said he was an administrator. However many schools he has built, it's a lot more than Jon Krakauer has.*

Potshots

Mortenson is not alone. Al Gore, environmentalist, took grief for living in a large home and burning up more than his share of jet fuel. He did not appear to be living simply, in the tradition of Thoreau, and this was a problem for a lot of people. (Although he appears to have addressed this issue with his current Nashville home, which, though large, is powered by geothermal wells.)[17]

Kiran Bedi's personal narrative, despite the fact that she had been voted the most trusted woman in India, came into question when she faced allegations that she had fudged her travel expenses, particularly for speaking engagements, charging organizations full-price airfares when she purchased discount tickets, and business-class fares when she flew economy. Bedi adamantly denies that she personally benefited from these arrangements, and maintains that she reinvested the funds she saved into her chosen causes, which allowed her to speak to worthy organizations that otherwise could not afford her travel expenses.[18]

Even Thoreau has come under fire for mythologizing. Yes, he lived in that house in the woods, but it was only a mile from town, as the dis goes, so he wasn't all *that* isolated. He left the woods after a couple of years, so it wasn't that great a commitment. He was a Harvard graduate, a member of the elite, not the simple man of the earth that his character seems to suggest. He didn't have a family, so he didn't have to earn a living. It was all just an experiment and not a real life path.

Such doubts always arise about the genuineness of the myth that starts to build around the idea entrepreneur—and, like backlash, the doubts usually serve to further the myth. One simply has to make one's own judgment about whether the effort seems genuine and admirable. Large numbers of people have concluded that Thoreau's time in the woods was both of those things. It is something that most of us have not done and will not do, no matter how much we talk about the desire to "get back to the land" or "live simply." And although it was an experiment for Thoreau, and he says so, it doesn't seem like a gimmick.

Gandhi comes under fire, too, and his myth has been debated and dissected. What about his views toward women? About modern medicine? It is this life modeling that separates Gandhi from other social reformers, those who do not put their ideas as fully into practice as he did—the non–meat eater going so far as to prevent the doctor from giving his ill son chicken broth. Gandhi subtitled his autobiography *The Story of My Experiments with Truth*. Modeling is also what separates Cesar Millan from veterinarians whose ideas may be just as potent, but who do not get up at 5:30 every morning to run with as many as sixty-five dogs, and who did not sneak across the Mexican border to find the secret of Rin Tin Tin.

Again, I am not saying that the ideas of Thoreau, Gandhi, or Millan are better or somehow more right than others, just that they scintillate more because they are animated by personal example. It is their strength and also their weakness, since any straying from the path calls into question the value of the idea.

So, idea entrepreneurs need not be saints, but they have to be careful when they allow or enable their narratives to grow into myths. When the myth is contradicted by new developments in the narrative or by practices that don't seem to fit, the fascination, expression, and even the fundamental idea can come into question.

This seems like an obvious point, but this "walking of the talk" is the greatest lack for many would-be idea entrepreneurs, from the academic who wants to expound on an idea but has no intention of living it, to the consultant who wants to tell clients how to operate but has never done so himself. It's living the idea to a degree that very few people are willing to undertake.

Tangled Truth

The functioning of the brain also works its tricks in the making and distorting of myths and the iconic moments of the personal narrative. As the idea entrepreneur tells the story over and over again, and as more and more expressions are created around the story, it can become distorted, simplified, changed, and less and less connected to the original memory or the actual facts.

Ironically, although Hannah Salwen protested that she did not get involved in the Power of Half project as a way to gather material for her senior speech, it did end up as the subject of that speech—but not quite as one might expect. Hannah sent us the file of her speech, which I believe has not been published before. She starts off by sharing a synopsis of her favorite short story, "Good Form" by Tim O'Brien, and then explains why she has done so.

"I share this story with you," she said to her classmates when she delivered the speech before the entire school, "because I'm a storyteller. We all are. If you know anything about me, you probably think this speech will be about the long struggle of selling my house and moving into one half the size. It was hard and a difficult process but it brought our family together blah blah blah, and we lived happily ever after. But that's not what this speech is about."

Hannah goes on to distinguish between what she calls the "happening truth" and the "story truth" and the importance of iconic, or "defining," moments to both. "So, what's the connection between storytelling and defining moments?" Hannah asked, rhetorically. "I said earlier that I wasn't going to tell you the story of *The Power of Half*—the story of my family selling our house. But I am."

She then tells the story one more time. The fall of 2006. Coming home from a sleepover. Stopping at the red light. The homeless man. The guy in the Mercedes. "I've told this story publicly 437 times . . . I guess it's now 438. Every time I've told this story it's the same."

Then comes the key line.

"But the reality is," Hannah told her classmates, "I can't actually remember what happened at the stoplight that day with my dad. I had to create a truth within this story."

So it didn't happen? She was making the whole thing up?

"The story is true—I DID see a homeless man and a Mercedes and convince my family to sell our house and give half the money to villages 6,000 miles away. But the story is also enhanced: The details and the sequence of events of the story are made up. But it doesn't make the story any less true. What happened happened, but the way I tell it is made up, created for your consumption, created for speeches, created for a TV audience, created for entertainment.

"And it's made up for my own understanding too—because this is my story truth, the fictionalized truth that I am living. The fiction that is our reality."

This is the truth of every idea entrepreneur. They make an idea into a narrative and a narrative into an idea. It's true and also made up. It's up to us to decide whether it's true for us.

THE ENDURING SENTENCE

Over time, as the idea becomes associated with the idea entrepreneur, and as the narrative is passed along, simplified, retold, reinterpreted, and embellished, and the iconic moments and emblems gather more meaning and resonance, and as the expressions become classics and perennial sellers, the idea is gradually, inescapably boiled down until, at last, it is represented in our minds by a single sentence, a phrase, sometimes just a word or two. Fair or unfair, accurate or not, that's what happens.

It is this sentence that comes to count as the idea entrepreneur's key contribution to the thinking journey.

Efficiency

The Argentinean author Jorge Luis Borges (1899–1986) wrote a very short story called "The Mirror and the Mask" that makes a fable of the perils of coming up with a single sentence that captures the essence of any fundamental and powerful idea.

In the story, the High King of Ireland commands his court poet to write a verse to celebrate his country's victory in a recent battle. The poet scribbles and suffers for a year, then returns to court and declaims the verse to the king, who is well pleased and rewards the poet with a silver mirror. The king asks the poet to compose another, even more gorgeous, poem. The poet spends another year in solitude and comes back with a much shorter verse. "It was not a description of the battle," Borges writes, "it was the battle."[19] (Shades of Tolstoy: the audience must experience the emotion for themselves.) The king rewards the poet with a golden mask and then pushes things a little too far. He asks the poet to give it just one more go.

A year later the bard returns, shaken. He protests that he doesn't want to recite his new work, but the king insists. The verse is not a verse at all. It is a single line, terrifying in its beauty and perfection. After the poet reads the line, the king rewards the poet with a dagger with which he immediately stabs himself to death. The king gives up his throne and spends the rest of his life wandering his country as a beggar.

I don't know of any sentences that idea entrepreneurs have created—or have been created around them—that are of such perfection and beauty as to provoke suicide, but the efforts of the idea entrepreneur do tend to get boiled down into that phrase or sentence of such efficiency and durability and flexibility that it can carry meaning for a good long time.

Thoreau is associated with living deliberately, Gandhi with *satyagraha* or "truth firmness," and Emerson with self-reliance. We'll see how Cesar's "calm assertiveness," Hannah's "power of half," or Mireille Guiliano's "*joie de vivre* is the way to good health" fare.

Porosity

Of course, the sentence that lingers in the ideaplex may not be the one that lingers in the individual's mind. Ultimately, it is, or should be, a matter of the one-on-one effect. So although every idea may get reduced to a sentence, its meaning and value, its affect, ultimately is a matter of how that sentence resonates with you. Although Thoreau is a prototypical idea entrepreneur, a model for all who seek to start movements and make differences in this country, and the better-selling author than Emerson at the moment, I do not suggest that he is necessarily more influential or valuable, or make any judgment of that kind at all.

Emerson is hardly forgotten, after all, especially by other thinkers and idea-driven people. Mary Oliver, the Pulitzer Prize–winning poet, speaks for many, I'm sure, when she says that Emerson is very much inside her head. "There are, for myself, a hundred reasons why I would find my life—not only my literary, thoughtful life but my emotional, responsive life—impoverished by Emerson's absence," she writes in an introduction to a collection of Emerson's writings. "I think of him whenever I set to work on something worthy."[20]

Emerson knew this, too. Although he poked at Thoreau as an oddity and little more than "the captain of a huckleberry-party," Emerson understood that Thoreau was the genuine article. "No truer American existed," he wrote.[21] This is a critical point. The idea entrepreneur, the one who gains attention through the ideaplex and who becomes a part of our thinking, is not latching on to a fad, pretending to believe, yearning for the spotlight, consumed by self-love, or driven by commerce and profit. The idea springs from a deep personal fascination and tends to be lifelong. If they were booted out of their endeavor, they would not abandon their idea. "We are often reminded," Thoreau wrote in *Walden,* "that if there were bestowed on us the wealth of Croesus, our aims must still be the same."[22]

And, of course, Thoreau died relatively young, in 1862, at the age of forty-four, of tuberculosis. As a result, he didn't have time to fall into one of the many traps that can turn the genuine idea entrepreneur into something else—a statue of his former self, for example, or a tired regurgitator of his own ideas, caught up in a whirl of attention and separated from his original intentions. He is the James Dean of idea entrepreneurs.

Thoreau's staying power was predicted by at least one of his contemporaries, Franklin Sanborn, who knew and studied both Emerson and Thoreau. When Sanborn was asked by Walt Whitman, the poet, which of the men of Concord would "last into the future," Sanborn replied that it would be Thoreau.[23]

He was right and also wrong. They have both endured, but in different ways.

IDEAS ABOUT IDEAS

Of course, the lasting sentence may not be accurate, fair, complete, or even bear much resemblance to the idea entrepreneur's original idea.

This is in part because a great deal of respiration about an idea takes place without any direct contact with the idea entrepreneur or any of his expressions, but only through engagement with the expressions of others. People hear about the idea entrepreneur, know about the book, are aware of the television show and TED talk, have been told about the viral video, but have not personally been interested enough, or taken the time, to actually read the book or blog or whatever. That is, people learn about the idea only through second- or third-hand expressions.

An example. I mentioned to a friend in the publishing industry that I would be featuring Cesar Millan in this book. He paused. "But he's so . . . I mean . . . " He wrestled with what he did mean. "I just mistrust anybody who has that much exposure. He's *everywhere*." My friend stopped for a moment. "Of course," he said, remembering that he considers himself an enlightened consumer of ideas and is a member of the ideaplex himself, "I've near read anything he has written, or seen his show. I've just heard a lot about him."

Hannah Salwen became acutely aware of this phenomenon. In none of their expressions did the Salwens suggest that anybody else do anything quite so drastic as they had done. "People have really not understood that," she told us. "If you read the book, and if you watched a couple of the media clips, and didn't just read one article, then you would for sure know that."

But, of course, people didn't actually read the book and they did make their own assumptions about the project, and created their own expressions, based on what they heard or thought they heard. They had their own ideas about her ideas.

So, no matter how many expressions you create, no matter how many audience members you connect with directly or indirectly, that does not mean that people will feel the need to actually inspect your idea in any of its expressions in order to develop an opinion about it, pass it along to others, or put it into practice in the way they assume it is meant to be practiced.

Respiration includes all of this remote activity, as well, and it can be a source of frustration and complication for the idea entrepreneur. First-time entrants to the ideaplex, in particular, are disturbed when they come across the first misunderstanding or misrepresentation of their idea. This is what Hannah Salwen's mother, Joan, felt when she read the nasty comments on the *Today* show blog post about the Salwens. She wanted to rebut them, answer back somehow. But it's impossible. I have had clients who become outraged that a reporter in the *Wall Street Journal* or a commentator on a blog gets it so wrong.

Unread Totems

Without the original voice involved, the ideas about ideas can get pretty far from the original intention. *Walden* is still talked about and sells well, but that does not mean that it is widely read, completely read, or read at all. Some members of my research team had not read it before we began our work, although they of course knew about it.

It is not unusual for a breakout book to be an unread one. Bill McKibben says of *Walden* that "[u]nderstanding the whole of this book is a hopeless task," and John Updike agrees that Thoreau's sacred expression, because of the way it is written, is at risk of being "as revered and unread as the Bible."[24]

Walden is hardly the only revered book that is as much talked about as read. The author and academic Louis Menand, who writes about books and publishing, argues that the actual reading of such books is scarcely necessary for them to influence people's thinking. He cites such books as *The Feminine Mystique* by Betty Friedan (feminism), *The Death and Life of Great American Cities* by Jane Jacobs (urban renewal), *Silent Spring* by Rachel Carson (environmentalism), and Ralph Nader's *Unsafe at Any Speed* (auto safety) as works that become totems, vessels into which people imbue their own views on the topic (as they suppose the topic to be, even if it isn't).[25]

However, Menand argues, "the changes the books are associated with would have happened anyway." His article is partly a review of a book that explores Friedan, *A Strange Stirring: 'The Feminine Mystique' and American Women at the Dawn of the 1960s* by Stephanie Coontz. "But people like to be able to point to a book as the cause for a new frame of mind, possibly for the same reason that people prefer anecdotes to statistical evidence," Menand writes. "A book personalizes an issue. It has an Erin Brockovich effect: it puts a face on the problem; it sets up a David-and-Goliath drama."[26]

Menand argues that some books become "totems" and people stuff into them ideas that are not actually contained there. Menand cites *The Feminine Mystique,* which did *not* encourage women to cultivate full-time careers as some people thought, and *Silent Spring,* which did *not* suggest banning pesticides, which became conventional wisdom about the work, but rather argued for better regulation of them. This is not to say that no one read those books, because many did, and many were deeply affected by them.

Besides, it may be that, along with its totemic nature, the quality of being unread contributes to a book's popularity and longevity. While in Beijing in the summer of 2011, I asked several Chinese people about one of the most famous of Chinese cultural tomes, *Dream of the Red Chamber.* Everyone knew about it. Only one person I met had actually read it (although one of our guides had seen a television series based on it, which he had really enjoyed).

First-time authors and would-be idea entrepreneurs understandably do not like to think their books or articles may not actually be read. Some indulge in an understandable fantasy: that their book will not only be read, but read word for word and cover to cover. They even imagine that the reading will take place in a single impassioned sitting immediately upon receipt of the book, and that the content will be completely understood in precisely the way the author intended, and will be perfectly remembered and passed along to others. When I ask such optimistic authors when they themselves last engaged with a nonfiction book in this way, they look a little sheepish. *Not recently.* Ever? *Maybe, when I was in graduate school.* But probably not.

Rejected Thoughts

Emerson has an interesting comment to make about the phenomenon of how people read and don't read books, what they take from them, and why they believe they are valuable—which can be applied to all the expressions of the idea entrepreneur. Great books are not great, he argues, because their authors are geniuses whose ideas are more brilliant than anyone else's. Quite the opposite, he says: their books are *seen* as great precisely because they contain ideas that many others share, but have been afraid or unwilling or unable to express for themselves.

"To believe your own thought," writes Emerson, "to believe that what is true for you in your private heart is true for all men,—that is genius."[27] Most of us will not allow ourselves to think that our ideas are worthy of expression. Then we read a book in which "we recognize our own rejected thoughts: they come back to us with a certain alienated majesty."[28] *That is a great book,* we say to ourselves. *I couldn't have said it better myself.* The idea entrepreneur who speaks *for* us, rather than *at* us, is the one who achieves popularity, wide exposure, respiration, longevity, and influence.

THE NEED

Today, the impulse to start movements, make a difference, and create change in the world may have become a far stronger and relevant interpretation of the American dream than the one that has held sway for so long—that of home ownership, a rising income, a chance to climb some ladder of opportunity, and the assurance of a social safety net or two.

Although we may have an idea glut, I prefer that to an idea shortage. More and more people, especially young people, want to build lives like those of the idea entrepreneur. Plenty of kids may still dream of growing up to be presidents and superstars, of owning large quantities of material goods, but more and more of them want to find a way to pursue their own fascination, connect their personal narrative to a larger idea—ideally something that not only improves individuals and society as a whole but also allows them to earn a decent living and not work in a job they can't abide or for an institution they don't trust or respect. They want to be part of a thinking journey.

In the age of the ideaplex, in which we are surrounded by channels and activities that deliver unto us great platters of ideas each day, introducing an idea to the world can look much easier than it really is. John Kenneth Galbraith probably had it right when he said that we Americans sometimes seem to think that *saying* we value new ideas is the same as actually having them—recognizing them, embracing them, and putting them into practice.[29] No, as much as we are inundated by information every day, and as much as we wriggle with delight at the new new thing, the new idea that really takes hold is still a rarity. "Conventional wisdom" (which, by the way, comes from Galbraith's book *The Affluent Society*) is always hard to disrupt, transform, and augment, as all of the idea entrepreneurs in this book will attest.

But few would disagree that a great deal of that supposed wisdom needs to be dislodged in our society today—entrenched notions about education, justice, health, religion, relationships, business, and America's role in the world need to be rethought, reworked, replaced. Some of the new ideas may emerge through social media and the "wisdom of crowds," as James Surowiecki would have it, some may bubble up through businesses and institutions, and some will take the form of technologies or laws, but many will come from idea entrepreneurs—outsiders, individuals, mavericks who live and express their ideas—especially those that pertain to individuals and how they think, behave, and improve themselves and society.

Issues that concern how we eat, how we relate to others, how we give money away, how we relate to animals, how we connect with nature, how we work and manage work—these are things that largely cannot be legislated, or shifted through technology, or forced by power or organizational structure or any mechanistic method. They can only be touched through an alchemy of expression, suggestion, connection, emotions, stories, life models, and a welcoming thinking journey. These are the methods of the idea entrepreneur.

So, if we all have fascinations, revelations, and accumulations of stuff, does this mean that we can all create a sacred expression of our idea? Plant an idea in the minds of others?

Yes, probably. Although the scale may vary.

It's a question of whether the fascination will fascinate others, whether it has relevance to the world at the moment (can it surface a tension?), whether the ideaplex will find it of interest, and whether it has the capacity to create respiration. But all of that need not take place on the global stage. It can happen on a small scale—in a community, an organization, even in a family.

The Risk

Not long ago, I was contacted by a literary agent. He had an interesting client, he said, who wanted to write a book, create a platform, promote an idea, go public, and he needed some help.

"Aha. And who is this client? What is his or her idea? What does she want to say?" I asked.

"Well, it's a teenage boy." My agent gave me his name. "His fascination is science. He has invented a new energy device. He won a national award and spoke at various high-level conferences. He's a great kid. A genius. And he has a wonderful family supporting him."

I thought of Hannah Salwen at age fourteen and of Cesar Millan at age twenty-one. I thought of my father and his solar hot water heater.

Do they know what they are getting into? I wondered. But I agreed to have a conversation with them.

I spoke with the young man and his mother on the phone. It was a summer afternoon and he had been on the beach for hours, and he was also still young, so his attention wandered a bit from time to time.

I asked him how he felt about what he had already been through. He felt good, he said, although it had gotten weird at times. Some of his classmates thought he was getting a big head. His mother agreed that even some of their adult friends had been less than enthusiastic about his successes.

I wondered again: Why do they want to do this? Why do they want to disrupt people, challenge existing ideas, create these difficult expressions, model the practices every day, deal with the ideaplex, risk backlash and ridicule, all for the love of an idea?

Of course, there is no definitive answer to these questions.

But I'm glad that they do take the risk, do try to go public, do try to make a difference, start a movement, change the world—or at least some small part of it. Even when there are far too many ideas swirling around us, as there certainly are today, there are never enough really good ones, especially really good ones that have the good fortune to be associated with a person who is willing to break out—of her accustomed track, of the conventional way of thinking, of established structures—to bring the idea forward for our consideration, for our discussion, perhaps for our embrace, and even, we can hope, for the benefit of us personally and of the society we share.

THE TEST OF EFFECT

The idea entrepreneur usually can't know what his or her sentence will be, nor can they know where they will fit in the thinking journey or, ultimately, what effect they will have on society as a whole.

They tend, therefore, to evaluate their effort in one very simple way: the response they get from individuals. The in-person comments, written notes, e-mails and tweets, comments on blogs, testimonies at live events—most of them coming from people who are unknown to the idea entrepreneur—are usually the most meaningful and satisfying of all. This type of evaluation was mentioned with the most pleasure by all the idea entrepreneurs I spoke with. The testimonies and stories they hear directly from people, or indirectly about people who have been affected by their idea—*you changed my life*—tend to mean more than the book review or the appearance on a list of influential people.

Changed My Life

Today, much of this feedback comes from e-mails, postings on websites, or connections through social media sites such as Facebook. Years after the publication of *French Women Don't Get Fat,* Mireille Guiliano gets e-mails every day from people who have read her book. Some of them are "amazing and very moving," she told us, because they talk about how she "changed their life, and not only their life, but the life of their family." (Some of them are "nasty" too, she says. "You get criticized no matter what. You wouldn't believe what people write." Guiliano's assistant, who reads them all, says the nasty missives are probably one in a thousand.)

Before the advent of airborne connectivity, Guiliano would sometimes print out her e-mails so she could read them on a flight. She told us about one that came from a woman who wrote to say that she had attended a lecture Guiliano had given. The woman described how she had followed some of Guiliano's advice, which was pleasing for Guiliano to hear, but then came the part that really got to her. The woman related how, the previous Sunday, she had made a meal. "It was the first time in eight years I had used real dishes," she wrote. "I even put out a tablecloth, and I cooked a meal, and I couldn't believe that the kids and my husband, they loved the food, we had a real conversation." Guiliano could barely finish the letter. She kept thinking: *Oh my God, of course you will enjoy this lifestyle.* She started crying. The man in the seat next to her finally turned to her and asked if she was OK. "I said, yes, yes, yes." She kept reading and the next letter was funny and she couldn't help but burst out laughing at that one. "The man must have thought: *this woman is totally crazy.*"

Guiliano makes as many direct connections with her fans as she can. "People really want to meet you, and it's part of your responsibility. It's kind of overwhelming sometimes. You've got to stay focused and say, I'll do my best. But many people, I meet again after several years. They look good. And there's a snowball effect. They have given the book to their daughters or their friends." Then there are people I meet today who say, 'I just bought your book!' And I think, 'I wrote it six years ago!'"

Sometimes the meet-ups happen on the street. As she recounted in that e-mail, it happens to her in New York almost every day, even now. "Yesterday in the subway a young Swedish woman asks me how to go to the Met and as I was going there . . . to see the Alexander McQueen exhibit . . . so was she. We walked there together and started talking and finally she asked me what I do . . . 'author' I said and the next question is what do you write so obviously I mentioned FWDGF and the response is always 'No, you wrote THAT book' and so it goes."

That kind of direct contact and testimony has made Guiliano think even harder about her responsibilities as an idea entrepreneur. "Don't talk about eating healthy, if you're going to write cookbooks about eating pies and cupcakes and not mention what it does to your body." This is one reason that Guiliano has shied away from television, although she has had many offers to do a show.

Hannah Salwen also receives lots of e-mails. There have been the snarky negative ones, but a "huge" number have been positive, she told us. "People have said, this has changed the way that I'm looking at my life." An article in The *New Yorker* describes one of these e-mails, which read, "I have dreamed of living in a huge mansion and marrying a millionaire. But now, I see that the world is a largely connected community. I owe that to you. Today, I took out clothing from my closets that were too small or that I didn't wear . . . . You're making a difference!"[30]

"Do you think that the project—the book, all the media, the idea—has changed the way people think and the way that people

behave? Do you feel that it's created some kind of a movement?"
I asked Hannah.

"I do," she responded. "I don't know in how many people . . .
We just said, one is enough for us. But the e-mails that we've gotten and the responses that we've gotten—although a lot of them
have been negative—there have been a huge amount of positive
responses. And people have said, this has changed the way that
I'm looking at my life. So there is no doubt in my mind that it has
definitely changed some people. But the amount, I'm unsure of."

"How would you describe what the change is?"

"I would say it's definitely: be more conscious of what you
have, and what you're spending money on, what you're doing
with your time, just being more conscious of life. And realizing
that if you are one of the lucky ones, then knowing that you're
one of the lucky ones and not just sulking about what you don't
have and what you need."

It's important to note that one particularly influential individual, Bill Gates, took the Salwens' message to heart. As reported in
Forbes: "Gates is famous for asking other billionaires to commit to
giving away half their fortunes, reportedly inspired by Melinda's
reading *The Power of Half* by Kevin Salwen and his 14-year-old
daughter Hannah in 2010, about selling their home, giving half
the proceeds to charity, and buying one half the size for their
family."[31] Since then, Gates has joined Warren Buffett and many
other of our wealthiest citizens in The Giving Pledge, which,
according to its website, "is an effort to invite the wealthiest individuals and families in America to commit to giving the majority
of their wealth to the philanthropic causes and charitable organizations of their choice either during their lifetime or after their
death."[32]

Eckhart Tolle, too, regards direct testimony as proof of his affect.
He writes of *The Power of Now*: "It has reached several million

readers worldwide, many of whom have written to me to tell of the life-changing effect it has had on them. Due to the extremely high volume of correspondence I receive, I am regretfully no longer able to send personal replies, but I would like to take this opportunity to express my deepest gratitude to all those who have written to me to share their experiences. I am moved and deeply touched by many of those accounts, and they leave no doubt in my mind that an unprecedented shift in consciousness is indeed happening on our planet."[33]

Made a Difference

Have the idea entrepreneurs I've written about changed my life? I like to test the idea entrepreneur's affect on myself and on members of our research team. What idea has Guiliano, for example, planted in my head? How has she influenced my thinking? Has she affected my behavior? No doubt. *Don't eat so fast. Take full notice of what you're eating.*

And how does that personal affect connect with a larger issue? Although I think of myself as a mindful eater, I still feel the American impulse when it comes to food. *Clean up your plate. Don't waste food. How about all those starving kids in [insert hungry country of your choice]?* Somehow, the act of eating got connected with goodness. Now our entire country is looking like *un sac de patates.* And so are France and Greece, and even the people of China and India are putting on weight.

Certainly, we need to make infrastructural changes, and there are many voices sounding there—some looking at legislation, some at technological solutions and other means. But the idea entrepreneur plays an important and different role by animating the issue, putting a human face on it. If Guiliano were to declare, "Obesity is an urgent national problem, you must change your lifestyle immediately so that you get thin," she would likely be ignored. But for her to say, "I have been fat and I know how painful and destructive it is personally, but I found a way to solve the problem that I would like to tell you about," is a very different thing.

Anna, too, says that Guiliano has affected her thinking and behavior. (Note: Anna is not fat, either.) "I consider what I'm eating and how much I'm enjoying it more than before—whether the ingredients are fresh, ripe, well combined." Guiliano has also entered Anna's thinking about exercise. "I've tried to build walking into my day," she said.

In short, when Anna finds herself with some kind of food-related situation—what to eat, how much, when, whether—she asks herself: *What would Mireille do?*

How about Edward Tufte? The practice I remember most vividly from Tufte's work is that all the information required for understanding information in a visual should be in one place. Forget about keys and legends; they're confusing and confound the gathering of meaning. The whole story should be available in the scope of a glance.

Tufte's work, too, connects to issues of greater importance. He believes that our ability to understand our complex world is helped or hindered by how information is presented visually. In a world that has fallen deeply in love with data, it took Tufte to show that data is only as good as our ability to present it visually.

I had a similar response to Cesar Millan. My family had a seventeen-year-old English setter named Dominic who had pretty much come to rule the household. More than once I thought to myself, *What would Cesar do?*

I asked the same question one day when I went for a bike ride and had a disconcerting interaction with a dog. I was pedaling along a country lane when I approached a yard where an unleashed dog was running about. As soon as he became aware of me, he began to growl and bare his teeth. The dog's owner grabbed his collar and I rode by. "He just doesn't like bikers," the owner called out to me, cheerily. A moment later, thinking I was clear of danger, I heard panting and the sound of paw nails scritching on pavement. I turned to see that the dog had escaped the owner's grasp and, teeth bared, was closing in on my ankle. I accelerated and escaped, thinking, what is wrong with those *people*, not, what is wrong with that *dog*.

These affects are not earth shattering, but they can be life changing, and they can add up—person by person.

WHO KNOWS?

Breaking out need not occur on a grand scale, nor must it involve a best-selling book or a star turn at the *Fortune* Most Powerful Women Summit (at least not at the beginning) to be rewarding to the idea entrepreneur, meaningful to other people, and worthwhile to a larger group, even society as a whole.

I did not fully appreciate or understand this until I met Maria Madison. Her story brings us back to Concord, where we began. Madison, like Thoreau and Emerson (and me), is a citizen of Concord. She is a more recent arrival, and African American; Concord's black population is about 5 percent of the total, less than the national average. Madison's husband is Jewish, so their two children are biracial and Jewish. When Madison and her family were considering moving to town, she was concerned about how her children would fit in at school. She went to visit a school administrator and asked, "What kind of diversity will we find here?" The administrator pulled a book off the shelf called *Concord: Its Black History 1636–1860*, privately published by the

Concord Public Schools. "That immediately drew me in," Madison said.

Then, not long after settling into their house, came Madison's iconic moment. She was driving to a soccer party. As she turned onto Bristers Hill Road, Madison noticed a plaque that read: *Scipio Brister Slave freed before 1772 lived near here.* (His real name was actually Brister Freeman, not Scipio.) She became fascinated with the legacy of Africans, especially freed formerly enslaved Africans, in this area. Gradually, her fascination grew into an idea: that Concord's character is as much shaped by Africans as it is by the Transcendentalists (Emerson and Thoreau). The fascination was not new to her; she had long been fascinated by the role Africans had played—if any—in predominantly white places, especially small towns, like the small Midwest town where she grew up.

Nor was the fascination unique to Madison. She soon connected and bonded with others—including some involved with Metco, a state-funded grant program designed to enable city students to attend community schools outside the city—who shared her interest. She and two friends began to accumulate material, read other works, and to identify and learn about places, homes, and locations where early African townspeople had lived or worked or fought and died. The three began giving walking tours of the sites they had identified, and continued gathering information and stories. People responded, started talking about the houses. Respiration had begun.

Madison and her colleagues knew they needed some form of expression and considered using the book *Concord: Its Black History*, which had the advantage of having been written by a teacher in the Concord Public Schools, and it detailed much of the history that Madison's group had been exploring. But the book was dated and incomplete, the idea was not powerfully enough expressed, and the author's narrative was not Madison's narrative.

Then they had an idea. The fascination lay in the houses and locations, and the narrative emerged from the objects and the landscape. They decided that the best form of expression, as well as the most useful, would be a map upon which all the relevant sites would be identified.

With the help of a volunteer graphic designer, Madison and her team created an illustrated map that depicts the town of Concord in a new way. Interspersed among the traditional sites—the ones associated with Emerson, Thoreau, and Concord's other famous authors, as well as the Old North Bridge and more sites associated with the first battle of the Revolution, Concord's other claim to fame—the map shows dozens of places where Africans lived, worked, and made their mark on the town. It was a revelation for many of us who live in town and the thousands who visit here each year.

Not only did the map animate the African experience, it was also a useful tool that facilitated a simple practice: when you walk around the town where you live (any town, any city), think about who and what was there before you. It may change how you think about your home place.

The walking tours and the map gained such an enthusiastic response that Madison and her friends created a not-for-profit organization, which they called the Drinking Gourd Project, whose purpose was to raise funds to support their work. The mission of the organization, according to the website, is to "shine a light" on Concord's "African and Abolitionist history from the 17th through the 19th centuries." The goal is to make this history "more accessible to residents and visitors in a way that will add a new layer to our understanding of our past and a deeper appreciation for the complexity of Concord and its role in creating a diverse America."[34] The drinking gourd is another name for the constellations of the Big and Little Dippers—which contain the North Star—that showed the way for people traveling in the Underground Railroad network.

Unexpectedly, an emblem emerged. One of the oldest, tiniest houses in Concord was slated for demolition. It turned out to have been the home of Peter Robins, the son of Caesar Robins, an African Revolutionary War veteran and one of the earliest known freed slaves in Concord. Three or four generations of his descendants had lived in the home, including one who hosted Concord Female Antislavery Society meetings at the house.

The Robins house became the emblem for the idea, and proved to have the same kind of visceral draw that Thoreau's house has for people. Generous donors came forward to fund the purchase of the house. The town of Concord offered it a plot of land. One fine spring day, the house was moved slowly along a country road to its new site not far from the Old North Bridge, the site of one of the first battles of the Revolutionary War.

With a genuine fascination, an accumulation of material, a map as an expression, a house as an emblem, and a tiny, volunteer institution, Madison and her colleagues—who include preservation and landscape architects, archivists, archeologists, dendrochronologists (experts in tree-ring dating), paint analysts, graphic artists, exhibits experts, and historians—have started a minor movement, without intending to. "We were just women who wanted to tell the story of Concord's African and abolitionist history," Madison told me. She does not exactly wish to change Concord. She does, however, want the African narrative to be part of "the natural landscape" of the town, as she put it. She has done that for me and many others—but it took a sacred expression and her personal narrative, and three years of work to make it happen.

Who knows where this idea, or any idea for that matter, might lead—what feelings it might hand on to others, what minds it might plant itself into, what infecting it might do, how it might influence thinking and behavior, what change it could bring, what difference it might make, what good it could do for the world?

A NOTE ON
METHODOLOGY

People take an almost uncanny interest in how books get written. Where does the author sit? Does he write in longhand? At what time of day? Does she have a bottle of bourbon at her elbow? How do iPads figure in? How often does she check e-mail? There are notions, which are not entirely off base, that writing should be done in a solitary location with a view of a rolling landscape.

Vladimir Nabokov, author of *Lolita*, wrote his books on index cards and shuffled the scenes around. You can see some of the cards at his boyhood home, which is now a museum of sorts, in St. Petersburg.

Anthony Trollope, Victorian-era author of forty-seven novels, wrote for three hours each morning.[1] If he finished a novel before the three hours were up, he'd pick up a new sheet and start on the next book.[2]

Mireille Guiliano, author of *French Women Don't Get Fat*, told me that she locked herself in a room on the isle of Sardinia with her computer, and the book "just spilled out."

David Milch, the creator of *NYPD Blue* and other television shows, sometimes "writes" by lying on his back and speaking dialogue, which an assistant enters into a computer; the lines then appear on a screen suspended over Milch's head.[3]

On the assumption that my creative process might be spurred by disrupting long-followed routines (desk, chair, computer), I thought I might write this book in some alternative way, perhaps aboard my sailboat in Mackerel Cove, on Bailey Island, Maine. I went aboard one day and sat below in the little cabin, my hair brushing against the deckhead, and felt the boat rock back and forth. Although I am not prone to seasickness, motion nausea is another matter. I abandoned that method.

I did write a little on the iPad, sometimes in bed at night. It was good for the early stages, when thoughts came in fragments. But when it came to the heavier lifting, I returned to the computer.

Gradually, I relearned what I already knew, which is that the specific method is less important than the state of mind it produces. It is necessary to find one's way into the writing trance, during which the writer and the page become one. Time flies by. The words do not resist.

This happened best when sitting in a second-floor alcove in our summer cottage on Bailey Island, looking over the lawn, which ends at cliff's edge with a view of Casco Bay. I believe it was Proust who said that a middle-distance view works best for writers. Not close enough to present distracting details. Not so gorgeous as to overshadow the interior scene. When the summer waned, fall drew to a close, and the cold overpowered our little wood stove, we returned to Concord and I finished the writing in my study there. Henry David Thoreau, who plays a role in this book, had lived just down the street, a century and a half earlier.

ABOUT THE COLLABORATION

Although I did the actual writing alone, that does not mean no one else was involved in creating the book. Far from it. It was a collaboration involving a team of nine people, each of whom brought a distinctive skill and viewpoint to the effort, as well as a range of life experiences and personalities. More than one of them appear in the book, and I have recognized them all in the acknowledgments.

A comment or two about this collaborative method, because I have been involved in much discussion over the years about the process. The first issue is that of stereotype. In this country, the minds of educated people seem to collectively become infused with the image of the writer as a solitary, garret-ensconced creature for whom the placement of every word is a near-religious act. Images of Dickinson and Proust come to mind, and possibly Jonathan Franzen. These are people, so the stereotype would suggest, unsullied by the commercial aspects of publishing and unconcerned with the response of an audience. Let us add Keats and perhaps Flaubert to that group.

Still, rather than try to negate the stereotype, because I think there is validity to it, I would rather like to distinguish the writing of poetry and fiction, and other works of imagination, from the creation of nonfiction works, especially those that are meant to be of some practical use to the reader, as this book is.

Here, the collaborative, team-based approach—with the lead author supported by associates and research assistants, and the work contributed to and reviewed by colleagues and other peers—is typical. The author is careful to describe his or her methods and acknowledge all contributors. This approach is often followed by the creators of nonacademic nonfiction, including works of history, biography, science, and business.

For this book, I worked with a loosely organized team, some of whose members came and went to various destinations, over a period of nearly four years. They contributed in a number of ways, including conducting research, writing background papers, participating in discussion sessions, and reviewing drafts.

An important part of the research was conducting the interviews with idea entrepreneurs whose stories are featured in the book (and some whose stories do not appear but will no doubt be useful in some other expression). I interviewed Russell Eisenstat and Maria Madison in person in the Boston area. Anna and I interviewed Mireille Guiliano, Roger Nierenberg, and Hannah Salwen, in person in New York City. (John Landry also conducted an in-person interview with Mireille Guiliano, in New York City.) Anna and I interviewed Blake Mycoskie and Cesar Millan on the phone. In Beijing, my wife Nancy and I, with our guide and interpreter Mia Li, interviewed Dai Qing, and Anna joined us for an interview with Ruqing Yang; both took place in person. In Delhi, Anna, Mridu Khullar Relph, and I interviewed Dr. Kiran Bedi, Anita Jha, Dr. Bindeshwar Pathak, and Belinda Wright in person. Clara Silverstein interviewed Bryant Terry by phone, and attended his lecture at Yale. John Landry conducted the interview with Dr. Andrew Weil, by phone.

Once the team had conducted these interviews and completed the period of accumulation, I reverted to stereotype and wrote the manuscript myself. So this book, like many others, is a hybrid— the product of many minds and contributors, distilled, synthesized, and expressed through the minds and fingers of one author, me.

ABOUT SALES DATA

As one indicator of the success and influence of the people I profile in this book, here and there I mention the sales figures of their published works. Except where otherwise indicated, the source of this data is BookScan U.S., a subscription service provided by Nielsen, a company that tracks and measures many aspects of the consumer, media, and retail environment in the United States and around the world. According to the Nielsen website, BookScan provides "continuous market measurement of U.S. retail book sales based upon electronic sales data analysis, and [we collect] point-of-sale information from a variety of retailers. In a typical week, sales of more than 300,000 different titles are collected, coded and analyzed, producing a complete market picture for retailers, publishers and the media."[4] It currently does not track e-book sales or purchases made by wholesalers or libraries, and only started reporting sales through Walmart in 2013.

BookScan data is useful, but has limitations. It is generally acknowledged that BookScan data does not account for all print books sold in the United States; rule of thumb is that it reflects about 70–80 percent of sales. We have tested this assertion by comparing BookScan data for some of our own books against the publisher's quarterly statements for those books, which, theoretically anyway, are based on the publisher's internal data and should be the most accurate accounting of sales. For the most part, we found that the BookScan number was, indeed, about 75 percent of the publisher's number. However, in some cases, the numbers varied substantially, with the BookScan number much lower than the publisher's statement. Colleagues in the publishing industry, particularly literary agents, have less faith in Nielsen data and argue that the sales figures BookScan reports are almost always low and generally not to be fully trusted.

In addition to this issue of accuracy, BookScan has two other limitations. First, its data starts in 2001, so it is very difficult, if not impossible, to determine how a book sold before that date. Second, while BookScan reports U.S. print sales data, many books with strong sales in the United States are translated and sold in other markets and can do very well there. We do not include sales from markets outside the United States in our figures.

Publishers track sales data for their own books, of course, but they typically don't share it with the world, especially for books that do not meet expectations. For very successful books, publishers will sometimes publicize a sales number, but even that can be a little misleading. Often it is the number of books "in print," which is not the same as the number sold.

Records of book sales before the widespread use of electronic sales collection methods (e.g., bar codes) are extremely spotty and unreliable. We're talking about clerks handwriting the record of a sale on a 3" x 5" card and publishers recording data in ledgers stored in safes. We can assume that reported sales figures in the twentieth century are estimates and those in the nineteenth century are largely guesses or legends.

So, despite these caveats and limitations, BookScan remains the best source of book sales data for the United States, and I have used it because it at least suggests the magnitude of sales for each book and enables comparison of one book to another. As I discuss, even accurate sales figures provide only one way to evaluate the success of a book. Some books sell a small number of copies that are avidly read and the ideas within them are widely discussed. Other books sell millions of copies and bring no ideas to the table at all. So please consider the data for what it is worth and take it with a grain of salt.

ACKNOWLEDGMENTS

I am full of gratitude for all the help, wisdom, guidance, analysis, insight, and information that has been contributed by so many people in the creation of this book.

I begin with thanks to those I have worked with, for, and in partnership with over the years, who have provided the greatest understanding of the trials of developing ideas, creating expressions, going public, and trying to break out. I have helped them in their efforts, observed them as they progressed, and discussed with them the issues involved.

Thanks to those idea entrepreneurs with whom I have not directly worked, but were kind enough to talk with me or members of my research team for this book, including Dr. Kiran Bedi, Russell Eisenstat, Mireille Guiliano, Anita Jha, Suzanne Lowe, Maria Madison, Cesar Millan, Blake Mycoskie, Roger Nierenberg, Dr. Bindeshwar Pathak, Dai Qing, Hannah Salwen, Bryant Terry, Dr. Andrew Weil, Ruqing Yang, and Belinda Wright.

Thanks to members of the project team. First among these is Anna Weiss, who has played many roles: as team member, project manager, researcher, editor, segment writer, thought partner, and companion in many of the adventures involved in the making of this book. She has made a major contribution to the work and been an invaluable boon to my ability to develop and write it. Other key members of the team were researcher-writers Hannah Alpert-Abrams and Janine Liberty, intern Julia Pressman, and Patricia Lyons, our office manager and moral supporter.

Thanks also to the independent participants on our team, including Barbara Lynn-Davis, John Landry, Clara Silverstein, and Mark Brown. In India, we received help from Mridu Khullar Relph and Meena Vadyanathan. In China, Ian Johnson helped us understand the nature of idea entrepreneurship there and made valuable connections for us. Mia Li served as our guide and interpreter in Beijing and Fangdei Chen assisted us from Shanghai. Thanks to Ollie Hallowell, who read an early version of the manuscript, and Rob Lachenauer, who gave valuable feedback on early chapters.

I thank my publishing team, particularly my editor at Harvard Business Review Press, Melinda Merino, who fulfilled the role that an editor truly should, but so few editors do, as a true shaper and guider of the book. Melinda has not only a deep understanding and appreciation of the struggles of being an author, but also a sense of humor about managing them. Given how much she improved the book from first draft to final, I have to wonder now what she really thought when she read the first go-round. I thank all of Melinda's colleagues at HBRP, especially Stephani Finks, design director, who took the time to talk at length about design and created a cover that immediately delighted everyone. Many thanks to my agent, Jacque Murphy, who helped me prepare the proposal and place the book with Harvard.

Thanks to my family for bearing with me, as always, during the creation of the book. My sons played a particularly interesting role, engaging with me on specific issues that influenced my thinking substantially. My older son, Jeremy, who is working toward his doctorate in philosophy, put me on to Nietzsche's *The Gay Science*, which provided the context of life affirmation for the idea entrepreneurs, as well as Alain Badiou's *Being and Event*, which got me thinking in a new way about normatives. My younger son, Henry, has steeped himself in the works of Thoreau and Emerson and he, like me, has been more deeply "infected" by the thoughts of Emerson than by those of Thoreau, and our discussions about the two helped me think through the nature of the influence of the two men, particularly in relation to their perceived popularity.

Thanks to my wife, Nancy, who followed her usual and extremely helpful mode of operation: discussing the project when it needed to be discussed, but not when it didn't; offering her opinion and thoughts on the issues when she felt it was contributory or necessary; and enduring with humor and grace all the usual trials and tribulations of living in the same life with a person who is writing a book.

Finally, I want to acknowledge my father, who died during the early stages of the book's development. He had many insights and ideas that he never minded talking about, even if he didn't choose to break out with them. I had always hoped to publish a book in which he would appear and that would recognize his contribution. I didn't quite achieve that goal, so this acknowledgment will have to do.

NOTES

CHAPTER 1

1. "The World Factbook: United States: People," *Central Intelligence Agency*, October 4, 2012, https://www.cia.gov/library/publications/the-world-factbook/geos/us.html.

2. David Hall, "The Uses of Literacy in New England, 1600-1850," in *Printing and Society in Early America*, ed. William L. Joyce, 2nd ed. (American Antiquarian Society, 1983), 2.

3. Robert D. Richardson Jr, *Emerson: The Mind on Fire*, first paperback ed. (Berkeley: University of California Press, 1995), 545.

4. Friedrich Nietzsche, *The Gay Science: With a Prelude in Rhymes and an Appendix of Songs*, translated by Walter Kaufmann, (New York, NY: Vintage Books-Random House, 1974), 73.

CHAPTER 2

1. Cesar Millan and Melissa Jo Peltier, *Cesar's Way: The Natural, Everyday Guide to Understanding and Correcting Common Dog Problems* (New York: Three Rivers Press, 2006), 24.

2. "About the Book: French Women Don't Get Fat," Mireilleguiliano.com, http://mireilleguiliano.com/fr/frenchwomen.htm.

3. Mireille Guiliano, *French Women Don't Get Fat*, (New York: Knopf, 2005), 18.

4. Alan Cowell, "Garret FitzGerald, Ex-Irish Premier, Dies at 85," *New York Times*, May 19, 2011, sec. World / Europe, http://www.nytimes.com/2011/05/20/world/europe/20fitzgerald.html.

5. Richard McKeon, ed., *The Basic Works of Aristotle* (New York: Modern Library-Random House, 2001), 1461–1463.

6. Abraham H. Maslow, *Toward a Psychology of Being* (New York: John Wiley & Sons, 1999), 5 and 31–33.

7. Stephen R. Covey, *The 7 Habits of Highly Effective People: Powerful Lessons in Personal Change* (New York: Fireside, 1989), 11.

8. Dan Schawbel, "Stephen R. Covey Revisits the 7 Habits of Highly Effective People," *Forbes*, September 1, 2011, http://www.forbes.com/sites/danschawbel/2011/09/01/stephen-r-covey-revisits-the-habits-of-highly-effective-people/.

9. Benjamin Franklin, *The Autobiography of Benjamin Franklin* (Stilwell, KS: Digireads.com Publishing, 2005), 52.

10. Ibid, 53.

11. Ibid, 52–53.

12. Daniel Kahneman, Dan Lovallo, and Olivier Sibony, "The Big Idea: Before You Make That Big Decision . . ." *Harvard Business Review*, June 2011, http://hbr.org/2011/06/the-big-idea-before-you-make-that-big-decision/ar/1?conversationId=1658396.

13. "Greatest Good." Greatestgood.com, http://www.greatestgood.com/#.

14. Boogie Down Productions, "Beef," Edutainment (Zomba Recording LLC, 1990).

15. Bryant Terry, "A Day for Dr. King with Bryant Terry, Activist, Author, and Chef" (Yale University, January 18, 2010).

16. Ibid.

17. Ibid.

18. Ibid.

19. Ibid.

20. Deborah Shapley, "The Da Vinci of Data," *New York Times*, March 30, 1998, http://www.nytimes.com/1998/03/30/business/the-da-vinci-of-data.html?pagewanted=all&src=pm.

21. Adam Aston, "Tufte's Invisible Yet Ubiquitous Influence," *BusinessWeek*, June 10, 2009, http://www.businessweek.com/innovate/content/jun2009/id20090610_157761.htm.

22. Ibid.

23. Alan Bisbort, "Escaping Flatland," *Hartford Advocate*, October 1999, http://www.edwardtufte.com/tufte/advocate_1099.

24. Edward R. Tufte, *Visual Explanations: Images and Quantities, Evidence and Narrative* (Cheshire, CT: Graphics Press, 1997), 10.

25. Adam Aston, "Tufte's Invisible Yet Ubiquitous Influence."

26. "Presenting Data and Information: A One-Day Course Taught by Edward Tufte," Edwardtufte.com, http://www.edwardtufte.com/tufte/courses.

27. Mohandas K. Gandhi, *An Autobiography: The Story of My Experiments with Truth* (Boston, MA: Beacon Press, 1993), 111–112.

CHAPTER 3

1. William Yardley, "Zig Ziglar, Motivational Speaker, Dies at 86," *New York Times*, November 28, 2012, http://www.nytimes.com/2012/11/29/business/zig-ziglar-86-motivational-speaker-and-author.html.

2. Leo Tolstoy, *What Is Art?*, trans. Aylmer Maude (New York: Penguin Classics, 2011), Kindle edition, location 769–771.

3. Ibid., location 771–772.

4. Ibid., location 768.

5. Ibid., location 774-775.

6. John Ruskin, *Modern Painters*, vol. 1 (of 5) (A Public Domain Book, Amazon Digital Services, Inc., 2006), Kindle edition, location 2285–2286.

7. Janet Maslin, "Vicarious Living: Power of Snob Appeal," *New York Times*, February 21, 2005, http://www.nytimes.com/2005/02/21/books/21crow.html.

8. Kevin Salwen and Hannah Salwen, *The Power of Half: One Family's Decision to Stop Taking and Start Giving Back* (New York: Houghton Mifflin Harcourt, 2010), 24.

9. Ibid., 24–25.

10. Ibid., 32.

11. Ibid., 88.

12. "Coldwell Banker Names Grand-Prize Winners of the Third Annual 'My Home: The American Dream' Contest," Coldwell Banker, February 4, 2008, http://www.coldwellbanker.com/real_estate/learn?learnPage=DETAIL&contentId=14455923&customerType=News.

13. "A Family's New American Dream," *Today* (NBC), http://www.msnbc.msn.com/id/21134540/vp/25568850#25568850.

14. Emily Hohler, "The Power of Half: How Hannah Salwen and Her Family Gave Half Their Home Away," *The Telegraph*, March 26, 2010, http://www.telegraph.co.uk/family/7527861/The-Power-of-Half-how-Hannah-Salwen-and-her-family-gave-half-their-home-away.html.

15. Nicholas D. Kristof, "What Could You Live Without?," *New York Times*, January 23, 2010, http://www.nytimes.com/2010/01/24/opinion/24kristof.html.

16. Kevin Salwen, "Meeting the Gates," *The Power of Half*, February 19, 2011, http://www.thepowerofhalf.com/Meeting-the-Gates.

17. "14-Year-Old Teaches Family the 'Power of Half,'" ABC News video (ABC, February 8, 2010), http://abcnews.go.com/WNT/video/14-year-teaches-family-power-half-9782067.

18. Oliver Burkeman, "The Bedsit Epiphany," *The Guardian*, April 11, 2009, http://www.guardian.co.uk/books/2009/apr/11/eckhart-tolle-interview-spirituality.

19. John W. Parker, *Dialogues With Emerging Spiritual Teachers* (Fort Collins, CO: Sagewood Press, 2009), 99.

20. Ibid., 99–101.

21. Douglas Todd, "Profile: Eckhart Tolle—Of the Present, Future and Mother," *Vancouver Sun*, October 5, 2002, sec. The Search, http://blogs.vancouversun.com/2008/10/16/profile-eckhart-tolle-of-the-present-future-and-mother/.

22. Eckhart Tolle, *The Power of Now: A Guide to Spiritual Enlightenment* (Novato, CA: New World Library and Namaste Publishing, 2004), 3.

23. Ibid., 3.

24. Ibid., 3–4.

25. Ibid., 5.

26. Todd, "Profile: Eckhart Tolle—Of the Present, Future and Mother."

27. Burkeman, "The Bedsit Epiphany."

28. Ibid.

29. Juli Cragg Hilliard, "Case Study 2: The Power of Wow," *Publishers Weekly*, August 23, 2004, http://www.publishersweekly.com/pw/print/20040823/38501-case-study-2-the-power-of-wow.html.

30. Constance Kellough, "About Namaste Publishing: A Visionary Mustard Seed—How Namaste Publishing Came into Being," Namaste Publishing, http://www.namastepublishing.com/about.

31. Ibid.

32. Hilliard, "Case Study 2: The Power Of Wow."

33. Ibid.

34. Ibid.

35. Daisy Maryles, "The Power of Oprah," *Publishers Weekly*, December 16, 2002, http://www.publishersweekly.com/pw/print/20021216/33219-the-power-of-oprah-.html.

36. Hilliard, "Case Study 2."

37. Emmie Twombly, "Power House," *Seventeen*, originally published in CosmoGirl, October 2006, http://www.seventeen.com/health/tips/martha-stewart-oct06.

38. Ralph Waldo Emerson, *The Collected Works of Ralph Waldo Emerson—Essays: Second Series*, ed. Joseph Slater et al., vol. III (Cambridge, MA and London, UK: The Belknap Press of Harvard University Press, 1983), xxiv.

39. James Elliot Cabot, *A Memoir of Ralph Waldo Emerson*, vol. II (Cambridge, MA: The Riverside Press, 1887), 383.

40. Ibid., 384.

41. Carl Bode, *American Lyceum: Town Meeting of the Mind. [1820's–1850's]* (New York: Oxford University Press, 1956), 222.

42. John Updike, *Due Considerations: Essays and Criticism* (New York: Ballantine Books, 2007), Kindle edition, location 3164–3165.

43. Cabot, *A Memoir of Ralph Waldo Emerson*, 479–480.

44. "Eckhart Tolle TV: About Eckhart Teachings," EckhartTolleTV.com, http://www.eckharttolletv.com/about/eckhart-teachings/.

45. Ken MacQueen, "Eckhart Tolle vs. God," *Maclean's*, October 22, 2009, http://www2.macleans.ca/2009/10/22/eckhart-tolle-vs-god/.

46. "GATE 2: Only a New Seed Will Yield a New Crop," Global Alliance for Transformational Entertainment, http://gatecommunity.org/gate2/.

47. N. S. Ramnath, "Decoding the Nobel Prize," *Forbes India Magazine*, October 11, 2012, http://forbesindia.com/article/cheat-sheet/decoding-the-nobel-prize/33865/0?id=33865&pg=0.

48. Michiko Kakutani, "Al Gore Revisits Global Warming, with Passionate Warnings and Pictures," *New York Times*, May 23, 2006, http://www.nytimes.com/2006/05/23/books/23kaku.html.

49. "emblem, n.", OED Online, http://oed.com/view/Entry/60880?rskey=jSZSvH&result=1&isAdvanced=false (accessed December 12, 2012).

50. Edward R. Tufte, *The Visual Display of Quantitative Information* (Cheshire, CT: Graphics Press, 1983), 40.

51. Salwen and Salwen, *The Power of Half*, 226.

CHAPTER 4

1. Kiran Bedi, *I Dare* (New Delhi: Hay House, 2009), 335–338.

2. Ibid., 339.

3. "India's Most Trusted People and Professions in 2010," *Punjab Newsline*, http://punjabnewsline.com/content/india%E2%80%99s-most-trusted-people-professions-2010.html.

4. Kiran Bedi, *It's Always Possible: Transforming One of the Largest Prisons in the World* (New Delhi: Sterling Publishers Private Limited, 2002), 3.

5. Ibid., 7–11.

6. "The 1994 Ramon Magsaysay Award for Government Service: Citation for Kiran Bedi," Ramon Magsaysay Award Foundation, August 31, 1994, http://www.rmaf.org.ph/Awardees/Citation/CitationBediKir.htm.

7. Ralph Waldo Emerson, *The Essential Writings of Ralph Waldo Emerson*, ed. Brooks Atkinson (New York: Modern Library, 2000), Kindle edition, location 8352–8359.

8. Robert D. Richardson Jr, *Emerson: The Mind on Fire* (Berkeley: University of California Press, 1995), 523.

9. Amy Chua, "Why Chinese Mothers Are Superior," *Wall Street Journal*, January 8, 2011, http://online.wsj.com/article/SB100014240527487041115045760597 13528698754.html.

10. "Our Readers Roar: What Makes a Good Parent," *Wall Street Journal*, January 15, 2011, http://online.wsj.com/article/SB1000142405274870395910457608187 3998873948.html.

11. *WSJ* Editor, "Permissive Western vs. Demanding Eastern: Which Style of Parenting Is Best for Children?" *Wall Street Journal*, http://online.wsj.com/community/groups/general-forum/topics/western-parents-too-indulgent.

12. Charles Murray, "Amy Chua Bludgeons Entire Generation of Sensitive Parents, Bless Her," AEI, *AEIdeas*, January 12, 2011, http://www.aei-ideas.org/2011/01/amy-chua-bludgeons-entire-generation-of-sensitive-parents-bless-her/.

13. Andrew Malcolm, "Donald Trump Has Read a Lot of Books on China: 'I Understand the Chinese Mind,'" Top of the Ticket: Political Commentary from Andrew Malcolm, *LA Times*, May 3, 2011, http://latimesblogs.latimes.com/washington/2011/05/donald-trump-i-understand-the-chinese-mind.html.

14. David Brooks, "Amy Chua Is a Wimp," *New York Times*, January 17, 2011, http://www.nytimes.com/2011/01/18/opinion/18brooks.html.

15. Sophia Chua-Rubenfield, "Why I Love My Strict Chinese Mom," *New York Post*, January 17, 2011, http://www.nypost.com/p/entertainment/why_love_my_strict_chinese_mom_uUvfmLcA5eteY0u2KXt7hM.

16. Evan Osnos, "Chinese Daughters and Amy Chua," *New Yorker Blogs, New Yorker*, January 11, 2011, http://www.newyorker.com/online/blogs/evanosnos/2011/01/chinese-daughters-and-amy-chua.html.

17. Martin Luther King, Jr., annotated by Michael Wilson, "16 April 1963: Letter from Birmingham Jail," the Martin Luther King, Jr., Research and Education Institute, April 16, 1963, http://mlk-kpp01.stanford.edu/index.php/encyclopedia/documentsentry/annotated_letter_from_birmingham/.

18. Amy Chua, "From Author Amy Chua," Amy Chua—Battle Hymn of the Tiger Mother, 2011, http://amychua.com/.

19. Leo Tolstoy, *What Is Art?*, trans. Aylmer Maude (New York: Penguin Classics, 2011), Kindle edition, location 772–773.

20. Kevin Salwen and Hannah Salwen, *The Power of Half: One Family's Decision to Stop Taking and Start Giving Back* (New York: Houghton Mifflin Harcourt, 2010), 210–211.

21. Shana, January 24, 2010 (10:53 a.m.) comment on Nicholas Kristof, "Giving Away Half a House," *New York Times*, January 23, 2010, http://kristof.blogs.nytimes.com/2010/01/23/giving-away-half-a-house/.

22. D, August 22, 2011 (5:22 p.m.) comment on Kevin Salwen, "Why We're Working Overseas," *The Power of Half*, January 22, 2010, http://www.thepowerofhalf.com/Why-were-working-overseas.

23. "Beyond Cesar Millan," http://beyondcesarmillan.weebly.com/.

24. "Who We Are," Pet Docs, 2009, http://www.thepetdocs.com/who.html.

25. Anna Bahney, "C'mon, Pooch, Get With the Program," *New York Times*, February 23, 2006, http://query.nytimes.com/gst/fullpage.html?res=990DE0DD1E3EF930A15751C0A9609C8B63&sec=&spon=&pagewanted=1&pagewanted=all.

26. Tufts Cummings School of Veterinary Medicine, http://vet.tufts.edu/facpages/dodman_n.html.

27. "How The Music Paradigm Works," The Music Paradigm, http://www.musicparadigm.com/about.aspx#how_tmp_works.

28. Elaine Sciolino, "Allegro, Andante, Adagio and Corporate Harmony; A Conductor Draws Management Metaphors from Musical Teamwork," *New York Times*, July 26, 2001, http://www.nytimes.com/2001/07/26/arts/allegro-andante-adagio-corporate-harmony-conductor-draws-management-metaphors.html?pagewanted=all&src=pm.

29. Kevin Salwen, "Year 2 of Power of Half Schools Starts Now," *The Power of Half*, October 18, 2011, http://www.thepowerofhalf.com/Year-2-of-Power-of-Half-Schools-Starts-Now.

CHAPTER 5

1. Dylan Tweney, "Tim Ferriss Takes Wired.com's Self-Promotion Prize," Wired.com, March 31, 2008, http://www.wired.com/business/2008/03/tim-ferriss-tak/.

2. "Speaking," The 4-Hour Workweek, http://fourhourworkweek.com/ferriss-speaking.htm.

3. Tim Ferriss, "Opening the Kimono to 200 People and Baring It All," *The Blog of Tim Ferriss*, April 12, 2011, http://www.fourhourworkweek.com/blog/2011/04/12/opening-the-kimono/.

4. "The Recovery Accountability and Transparency Board," Recovery.gov, http://www.recovery.gov/About/board/Pages/AdvisoryPanel.aspx.

5. Ibid.

6. Christie D'Zurilla, "Cesar Millan, 'The Dog Whisperer,' Reveals Suicide Attempt," *Los Angeles Times*, November 16, 2012, http://www.latimes.com/

entertainment/gossip/la-et-mg-cesar-millan-dog-whisperer-suicide-attempt-20121116,0,3097880.story.

7. Emmie Twombly, "Power House," *Seventeen*, originally published in *CosmoGirl*, October 2006, http://www.seventeen.com/health/tips/martha-stewart-oct06.

8. Martha Stewart Living Omnimedia Inc (MSO), "2011 Annual: 10-K Annual Report," March 6, 2012, http://phx.corporate-ir.net/External.File?item=UGFyZW50SUQ9NDU4MzEzfENoaWxkSUQ9NDg1NjU5fFR5cGU9MQ==&t=1.

9. Robert Slater, *Martha: On Trial, in Jail, and on a Comeback* (Upper Saddle River, NJ: Pearson Prentice Hall, 2006), 208–216.

10. James Surowiecki, "Sermon on the Mountain: How Edward Tufte Led Bose Out of the Land of Chartjunk," *Metropolis Magazine*, January 1999, http://www.metropolismag.com/html/content_0199/ja99ser.htm.

11. Jeff Zeleny, "As Author, Obama Earns Big Money and a New Deal," *New York Times*, March 19, 2009, http://www.nytimes.com/2009/03/20/us/politics/20disclose.html; Janny Scott, "The Story of Obama, Written by Obama," *New York Times*, May 18, 2008, http://www.nytimes.com/2008/05/18/us/politics/18memoirs.html.

12. Lois Romano, "Effect of Obama's Candor Remains to Be Seen," *Washington Post*, January 3, 2007, http://www.washingtonpost.com/wp-dyn/content/article/2007/01/02/AR2007010201359.html.

13. Scott, "The Story of Obama, Written by Obama."

14. Ibid.

15. Mike McIntire, "Clintons Made $109 Million in Last 8 Years," *New York Times*, April 5, 2008, http://www.nytimes.com/2008/04/05/us/politics/05clintons.html.

16. Holly Bailey, "What's Going on with Obama's Book Royalties?," Daily Beast, April 16, 2009, http://www.thedailybeast.com/newsweek/blogs/the-gaggle/2009/04/16/what-s-going-on-with-obama-s-book-royalties.html.

17. Tom Shine, "47% of Congress Members Millionaires—a Status Shared by Only 1% of Americans," *ABC News Blogs*, November 16, 2011, http://abcnews.go.com/blogs/politics/2011/11/47-of-congress-members-millionaires-a-status-shared-by-only-1-of-americans/.

18. Bailey, "What's Going on with Obama's Book Royalties?"; Jeff Zeleny, "As Author, Obama Earns Big Money and a New Deal."

19. Zeleny, ibid.

20. Nathaniel Cahners Hindman, "The Highest-Paid Public Speakers," *Huffington Post*, May 25, 2010, http://www.huffingtonpost.com/2010/05/25/the-highest-paid-public-s_n_588816.html#s93157&title=Bill_Clinton_150000450000; McIntire, "Clintons Made $109 Million in Last 8 Years."

21. Ryan Grim and Luke Johnson, "Mitt Romney Downplays $374,000 in Speaking Fees as 'Not Very Much,'" *Huffington Post*, January 17, 2012, http://www.huffingtonpost.com/2012/01/17/mitt-romney-not-much-definition-speaking-fees_n_1210522.html.

22. Cathy Lynn Grossman, "'Life's Purpose' Author Eckhart Tolle Is Serene, Critics Less So," *USA Today*, October 14, 2010, http://www.usatoday.com/news/religion/2010-04-15-tolle15_CV_N.htm.

23. jshortall (Jessica Shorthall), "Excited About . . . Parasites," *TOMS Shoes Blog*, March 4, 2010, http://www.tomsshoesblog.com/http:/www.tomsshoes-blog.com/excited-about-parasites.

24. Christina Binkley, "Charity Gives Shoe Brand Extra Shine," *Wall Street Journal*, April 1, 2010, http://online.wsj.com/article/SB10001424052702304252704575155903198032336.html.

25. "Warby Parker," http://www.warbyparker.com/.

26. "About The Weil Foundation," Drweil.com, http://www.drweil.com/drw/u/PAG00004/About-the-Weil-Foundation.html.

27. Ibid.

28. "Presence Through Movement," Omega, http://eomega.org/omega/workshops/361d812fdc26cfa1ad5ab2f180e2033d/.

29. Grossman, "'Life's Purpose' Author Eckhart Tolle Is Serene, Critics Less So."

30. "Eckhart Tolle TV: Learn More," EckhartTolleTV.com, http://www.eckharttolletv.com/learn/.

31. "Eckhart Tolle TV: Events," EckhartTolle.com, accessed April 18, 2012, http://www.eckharttolletv.com/event/.

32. Ken MacQueen, "Eckhart Tolle vs. God," *Maclean's*, October 22, 2009, http://www2.macleans.ca/2009/10/22/eckhart-tolle-vs-god/.

33. Grossman, "'Life's Purpose' Author Eckhart Tolle Is Serene, Critics Less So."

34. MacQueen, "Eckhart Tolle vs. God."

35. Grossman, "'Life's Purpose' Author Eckhart Tolle Is Serene, Critics Less So."

36. "Eckhart Tolle TV: Frequently Asked Questions," EckhartTolleTV.com, http://www.eckharttolletv.com/faq/.

37. "Deepak Chopra," IMDb, http://www.imdb.com/name/nm0159149/.

38. "Books: The 8th Habit Book Tools," Stephencovey.com, https://www.stephencovey.com/8thHabit/booktools/index.php.

39. "Stephen R. Covey," Stephencovey.com, accessed September 2012, https://www.stephencovey.com/.

40. Mridu Khullar, "Heroes of the Environment 2009: Bindeshwar Pathak," *Time*, September 22, 2009, http://www.time.com/time/specials/packages/article/0,28804,1924149_1924154_1924429,00.html.

41. V. S. Naipaul, *An Area of Darkness* (New York: Vintage Books, 2002), 75.

42. Mohandas K. Gandhi, *An Autobiography: The Story of My Experiments with Truth* (Boston, MA: Beacon Press, 1993), 404–405.

43. "Landmark Years in the Sulabh Sanitation Movement," Sulabh International Social Service Organisation, http://www.sulabhinternational.org/pages/landmarks_year_sulabh_movement.php.

44. Sulabh International Social Service Organisation, Sulabh Sanitation Movement (New Delhi), 5, 26.

45. Khullar, "Heroes of the Environment 2009: Bindeshwar Pathak."

46. Sulabh International Social Service Organisation, Sulabh Sanitation Movement, 4.

CHAPTER 6

1. Cesar Millan, "Before You Adopt a Dog," Cesar's Way, http://www.cesarsway.com/tips/yournewdog/Before-You-Adopt.

2. Mohandas K. Gandhi, *An Autobiography: The Story of My Experiments with Truth* (Boston, MA: Beacon Press, 1993), 318–319.

3. Clarence A. Manning, "Thoreau and Tolstoy," *New England Quarterly* 16, no 2 (June 1943), 234.

4. George Hendrick, "The Influence of Thoreau's 'Civil Disobedience' on Gandhi's Satyagraha," *New England Quarterly* 29, no. 4 (December 1956): 467.

5. Henry David Thoreau, *Walden* (Boston, MA: Beacon Press, 2004), Kindle edition, location 174.

6. Ibid., locations 1176, 1338, 3437, 3726.

7. Ralph Frasca, *Benjamin Franklin's Printing Network: Disseminating Virtue in Early America* (Columbia, MO: University of Missouri Press, 2006), 57.

8. Leonard A. Gordon, "Mahatma Gandhi's Dialogues with Americans," *Economic and Political Weekly* 37, no. 4 (January 26–February 1, 2002): 337, http://www.jstor.org/stable/4411660.

9. Walter Isaacson, *Benjamin Franklin: An American Life* (New York: Simon & Schuster, 2003), 478–479.

10. Harold Bloom, *Bloom's Classic Critical Views: Benjamin Franklin* (New York: Infobase Publishing, 2008), 79.

11. Ibid., 76.

12. Jon Krakauer, *Three Cups of Deceit: How Greg Mortenson, Humanitarian Hero, Lost His Way* (Byliner, 2011), location 212-216.

13. Ibid., location 243-245.

14. Ibid., location 249-253.

15. "Nobel Peace Prize Nominee Greg Mortenson to Repay Charity $US1 Million," News.Com, April 6, 2012, http://www.news.com.au/money/money-matters/nobel-peace-prize-nominee-greg-mortenson-to-repay-charity-us1-million/story-e6frfmd9-1226320478419.

16. Leslie Kaufman, "David Oliver Relin, Adventurous Journalist, Dies at 49," *New York Times*, December 2, 2012, http://www.nytimes.com/2012/12/03/business/media/david-oliver-relin-co-author-of-three-cups-of-tea-dies-at-49.html.

17. Patrick Healy, "The End of the Line," *New York Times*, August 25, 2012, http://www.nytimes.com/2012/08/26/fashion/the-end-of-the-line.html.

18. Kiran Bedi, "Wages of Fighting for a Cause," *Hindustan Times—Chandigarh*, October 29, 2011, http://kiran-bedi.blogspot.com/2011/10/wages-of-fighting-for-cause.html.

19. Jorge Luis Borges, "The Mirror and The Mask," trans. Norman Thomas di Giovanni, *New Yorker*, June 6, 1977, 34.

20. Ralph Waldo Emerson, *The Essential Writings of Ralph Waldo Emerson*, ed. Brooks Atkinson (New York: Modern Library, 2000), Kindle edition, location 205-207.

21. Ralph Waldo Emerson, "Thoreau," *Atlantic Magazine*, August 1862, http://www.theatlantic.com/magazine/archive/1862/08/thoreau/6418/?single_page=true.

22. Thoreau, *Walden*, location 3768.

23. Robert D. Richardson Jr, *Henry Thoreau: A Life of the Mind* (Berkeley, CA: University of California Press, 1986), 331.

24. Thoreau, *Walden*, location 33; John Updike, *Due Considerations: Essays and Criticism* (New York: Ballantine Books, 2007), Kindle edition, location 3115.

25. Louis Menand, "Books as Bombs," *New Yorker*, January 24, 2011, http://www.newyorker.com/arts/critics/books/2011/01/24/110124crbo_books_menand?currentPage=all.

26. Ibid.

27. Ralph Waldo Emerson, *Self-Reliance*, (C&C Web Press, 2009) Kindle edition, location 273–274.

28. Ibid, location 278–279.

29. John Kenneth Galbraith, *The Affluent Society* (Boston, MA: Mariner Books-Houghton Mifflin Company, 1998), 8.

30. Larissa MacFarquhar, "New Math," *New Yorker*, March 15, 2010, http://www.newyorker.com/talk/2010/03/15/100315ta_talk_macfarquhar.

31. Devin Thorpe, "The Real Reason the World Will Remember Bill Gates (Hint: It's Not Windows 8)," *Forbes*, September 5, 2012, http://www.forbes.com/sites/devinthorpe/2012/09/05/the-real-reason-bill-gates-the-world-will-remember-bill-gates-hint-its-not-windows-8/.

32. "The Giving Pledge: About," The Giving Pledge, http://givingpledge.org/#enter.

33. Eckhart Tolle, *The Power of Now: A Guide to Spiritual Enlightenment* (Novato, CA: New World Library and Namaste Publishing, 2004), xiii.

34. "Welcome," The Drinking Gourd Project, http://drinkinggourdproject.org/.

A NOTE ON METHODOLOGY

1. Hugh Walpole, "Anthony Trollope Had to Work by the Clock," *New York Times*, August 19, 1928, http://query.nytimes.com/mem/archive/pdf?res=F10A16F93B5E157A93CBA81783D85F4C8285F9.

2. Oliver Burkeman, "This Column Will Change Your Life," *The Guardian*, February 7, 2009, http://www.guardian.co.uk/lifeandstyle/2009/feb/07/health-wellbeing-advice.

3. Mark Singer, "The Misfit," *New Yorker*, February 14, 2005, http://www.newyorker.com/archive/2005/02/14/050214fa_fact_singer.

4. "Books & DVDs," Nielsen, http://nielsen.com/us/en/industries/media-entertainment/books-dvds.html.

INDEX

ABOUT THE AUTHOR

JOHN BUTMAN is a craftsperson of ideas and a worker in what he calls the ideaplex—"the wild, rich flow of real ideas" born not only of traditional and social media but of all the disparate activities, channels, structures, and venues involved in the creation, distribution, and consumption of idea-driven content. Trained in filmmaking at NYU's Tisch School of the Arts and the author of five books and many articles (his first published piece was a poem in *The Nation* magazine), John now works with content experts around the world, helping them develop and go public with their ideas in a variety of forms, from social media and apps to print books and videos. John has worked with leaders in universities and philanthropies, consultancies and businesses, as well as with independent professionals, and his work has taken him to some thirty countries. His clients and their ideas have been featured in dozens of publications—and bestseller lists—including the *New Yorker*, the *New York Times*, the *Financial Times*, the *Times of London*, the *Economist*, the *Independent*, the *Hindu*, and the *South*

Africa Times. They have also been featured in speaking venues worldwide, including The World Economic Forum at Davos, PopTech, and TEDx, and they have been included in the global Thinkers50 list. John is founder and principal of Idea Platforms, Inc., based in Cambridge, Massachusetts.